THE TALL BOOK OF

BIBLE STORIES

THE TALL BOOK OF
BIBLE
STORIES

RETOLD BY KATHARINE GIBSON

ILLUSTRATED BY TED CHAIKO

▉ HarperCollins*Publishers*

CONTENTS

THE OLD TESTAMENT

THE NEW TESTAMENT

THE OLD
TESTAMENT

THE CREATION

In the beginning God created the heaven and the earth. And the earth was without form or shape. Darkness was upon the face of the waters. And the Spirit of God moved upon the face of the waters.

And God said, "Let there be light."

And there was light. And God saw the light, that it was good. And God divided the light from the darkness. And God called the light Day, and the darkness He called Night. This was the first day.

And God said, "Let there be a sky in the midst of the waters and let it divide the water from the water."

And God called the sky Heaven. And God saw that it was good. This was the second day.

And God said, "Let the waters under the heaven be gathered together in one place, and let dry land appear."

And it was so; and God called the dry land Earth, and the waters He called the Seas.

And God said, "Let the earth bring forth grass, and the seeds of the field. Let the fruit tree bring forth fruit upon the earth."

This was the third day.

And God said, "Let there be light in the heavens to divide the day from the night, and let them be the signs for the seasons, the days, and the years."

And God made two great lights: the greater to rule by day, the lesser by night. He made the stars, also. And God saw that it was good. This was the fourth day.

And God made great whales and every living thing that moves through the waters, and every winged bird that flies above the earth. And God blessed them. And this was the fifth day.

And God said, "Let the earth bring forth living creatures, cattle and creeping things, and beasts of every kind."

And God created man in His own image. And God said to the man, "Behold, I have given you power over the fish of the sea and the birds of the air and over everything that creeps upon the earth, and over the beasts and the cattle of the field." And God said, "Behold, I have given you every herb-bearing seed which is upon the face of the earth, and every tree; to you it shall be for food."

And it was so. And God saw everything He had made; and behold, it was good. This was the sixth day.

Thus the heavens and the earth were finished. And on the seventh day God ended His work which He had done. And He rested on the seventh day. Then God blessed the seventh day and called it holy, because in it He had rested from all His work.

THE GARDEN
OF EDEN

And in the day that the Lord God made the earth and the heavens, He planted a garden eastward in Eden. In the light He planted it, and in the garden grew every tree that is pleasant to the sight and good for food. The tree of life was in the midst of the garden. And also in the garden was the tree of the knowledge of good and evil. Wide were its branches, and its fruit was round and smooth.

The Lord God created man in His image; out of the dust of the earth He created him. He put man in the garden to care for it and keep it. And the Lord God commanded the man, saying:

"Of every tree of the garden you may eat, but of the tree of the knowledge of good and evil you shall not eat, for on the day you eat of it you shall surely die."

And the Lord God said, "It is not good that the man should be alone; I will make a helpmate for him."

And out of the ground the Lord God formed every beast of the field and every fowl of the air. Dust became the song of the bird, the strength of the lion, the gentleness of the lamb, the fleetness of the deer, and the stealth of the red fox.

The Lord God brought all living creatures unto the man whose name was Adam to see what he would call them; and whatsoever Adam called every one, that was its name forever after. But Adam was alone; there was not found a helpmate for him.

And the Lord God caused a deep sleep to fall upon Adam, and he slept; and the Lord took one of his ribs, and closed up the flesh so there was no mark upon it. From the rib which the Lord God had taken from man, He made a woman, and brought her unto the man. And Adam said:

> *This is now bone of my bones,*
> *And flesh of my flesh;*
> *She shall be called Woman,*
> *Because she was taken out of Man.*

Therefore shall a man leave his father and his mother, and shall cleave to his wife, and they two shall dwell together.

From that day on, Adam and the woman lived in peace in the Garden of Eden. They did not have to hunt for food or till the soil. They were young and beautiful as the morning. They knew neither good nor evil. For like the stars and the fresh-flowing waters, they were but newly made.

Now, of all the animals that the Lord had made, the wisest and most crafty was the serpent. In that time, he walked like other beasts; and his voice was sweeter than honey and gentler than the doves. He spoke to the woman:

"Has the Lord God said, 'You shall not eat of every tree of the garden'?"

And the woman answered, "We may eat of the fruit of the trees in the garden, but not the fruit of the tree of the knowledge of good and evil. For God has said, 'You shall not eat of it, neither shall you touch it, or you shall die.' "

The serpent said unto the woman, "You shall not surely die, for God knows that in the day you taste of the fruit, then shall your eyes be opened and you shall be as gods, knowing good from evil."

The woman saw that the tree was good for food, and that it was pleasant to the eyes and a tree to be desired. For it would make her and Adam wise.

She took the fruit and ate of it.

She called Adam her husband to her, and gave also to him, and he ate. And the eyes of the two were opened, and they now had knowledge of good and evil.

Now they heard the voice of the Lord God, walking in the garden in the cool of the day. Adam and his wife hid themselves from the presence of the Lord God amongst the trees of the garden.

And the Lord God called to Adam and said unto him: "Man, come forth."

And Adam said: "I heard Your voice in the garden, and I was afraid, because I was naked."

And the Lord God said: "Who told you that you were naked? Did you eat of the tree which I commanded that you should not eat?"

And the man said: "The woman whom You gave to be with me, she gave me of the tree, and I did eat."

And the Lord God said unto the woman: "What is this you have done?"

And the woman answered: "The serpent tempted me, and I ate. His voice was sweeter than honey and more gentle than the doves."

The Lord God said unto the serpent:

> Because thou hast done this,
> Cursed art thou above all cattle,
> And above every beast of the field;
> Upon thy belly shalt thou go,
> And dust shalt thou eat,
> All the days of thy life.
> And I will put enmity between
>   thee and the woman
> And between her young and thine.
> He shall bruise thy head,
> And thou shalt bruise his heel.

Unto the woman He said:

> I will greatly multiply thy pain;
> In pain thou shalt bring forth children;
> And your husband shall rule over thee.

And unto Adam He said:

> Because thou hearkened unto the voice
>   of thy wife,
> And have eaten of the fruit of which
>   I commanded of thee,
> Saying, "Thou shalt not eat of it,"
> Cursed is the ground for thy sake,
> In sorrow shalt thou eat of it
>   all the days of thy life.
> Thorns also and thistles shall
>   it bring forth to thee,
> And thou shalt eat the herb of the field;
> In the sweat of thy face shalt thou
>   eat bread
> Till thou return unto the ground,
> For out of it wast thou taken.
> For dust thou art,
> And unto dust shalt thou return.

Now Adam named his wife Eve, which means first woman and mother of all the children of the earth.

And the Lord God said, "Behold, the man is become as one of Us, to know good and evil. And now, lest he put forth his hand and take also of the tree of life and eat and live forever, I will send him and the woman forth from the Garden of Eden."

And God drove them out, both the man and the woman. And Adam and Eve, sorrowing, went out together.

From that day forth, Adam toiled in the fields for all the bread that he and Eve did eat, they and their children. And Eve worked to spin and weave cloth that they might be clothed. And because they had eaten the fruit of which the Lord had commanded, "You shall not eat," never did Adam and Eve or any of the children of men return again to the garden. For at the east of the Garden of Eden the Lord God placed angels, and a flaming sword which turned every way to guard the tree of life.

NOAH'S ARK

Now as the days and years passed, the children of Adam and Eve and their children's children were many. They grew to be a great people; and they filled the earth. Because Eve ate the fruit of the tree which the Lord told her not to eat, and gave of the fruit to her husband Adam, all the children of men knew what things were good, and what things evil. But none in all the world did the things that were good, save one. His name was Noah.

And the Lord spoke to Noah:

"I will bring a flood of waters upon the earth; it will cover the valleys and the hills, even the mountains it will cover. Everything that is on earth will die, for the children of men have done those things which are evil. But build a boat, an ark out of gopher wood. You shall cover it with pitch inside and out. A window shall you put in the ark; the door shall you set in the side. With three stories shall you build it.

"I will make a covenant with you. You shall go into the ark, you and your wife, and your sons and their wives. And of every living thing, all the beasts of the field and birds of the air, you shall take two of every kind. They shall go into the ark. So shall they be alive with you.

"And you shall take food that is good for man, and food that is good for the beasts of the field, and food that is good for the birds of the air. And you shall gather it, and bring it into the ark that you may eat and not be hungry, and that the beasts and the birds shall not want."

Noah and his three sons, who were Shem, Ham, and Japheth, built the ark even as the Lord said. And Noah went into the ark, and his wife and his sons' wives. And the beasts of the field and the birds of the air went into the ark, two by two.

And after seven days had passed, the flood of waters was upon the earth. The fountains of the great deep opened up and the windows of heaven were opened. And the rain fell for forty days and forty nights. The waters lifted the ark from the earth. It floated upon the water. The waters covered the valleys and the hills, even the mountains were covered.

In all the world only Noah lived, and his wife and his three sons and their wives. In all the world only those beasts of the field and birds of the air lived that went into the ark two by two.

And the waters covered the earth for a hundred and fifty days. And the ark floated on the waters above the valleys and the hills, even above the mountains it floated.

And God remembered Noah and every living thing in the ark. He sent a wind over the earth. The fountains of the deep and the windows of heaven were stopped; the rains no longer fell. The waters grew less, and in the tenth month the tops of the mountains could be seen.

And it came to pass that Noah opened up the window of the ark which he had made. And he sent a dove out of the ark to see if the waters were gone off the face of the earth. But the dove found no rest for the sole of her foot; she came again to the ark, for the waters covered the earth. Then Noah put out his hand and took her again into the ark.

And Noah waited yet another seven days and sent the dove forth again. And the dove came to him in the evening, and in her mouth was an olive leaf she had plucked. So Noah knew the waters had gone from the earth.

The Lord spoke to Noah, "Go forth out of
the ark, you and your wife and your three sons,
Shem, Ham, and Japheth, and their wives with
them. And all the beasts in the ark, let them
come out; and all the birds of the air, let them
come out."

And Noah lifted the cover of the ark and
opened wide the door, and he and his wife and
his sons and their wives came once again to the
earth. And out of the ark, two by two, came all
the beasts, and all the birds of the air.

And Noah built an altar and prayed to the
Lord a prayer of thanksgiving.

And the Lord said:

"I will not again send the waters upon the earth, neither will I hurt any living thing. Forever shall there be seedtime and harvest, and cold and heat, and summer and winter, and day and night. So shall it be.

"And I shall make a covenant with you and with your wife, with your three sons and with your sons' wives. And I shall make a covenant with every beast of the field and every bird of the air that was in the ark. This is the sign. I will set a rainbow in the cloud. It shall be the sign of a promise between you and Me. And when I bring the clouds, I will also bring the rainbow And I will remember the promise between God and every creature of the earth."

And Noah and his wife, and his three sons and their wives, lived upon the earth. They cared for the fields, and the beasts of the field and the birds of the air. When the rain fell, and the clouds came, the Lord sent the rainbow. It was the sign of his promise to all living creatures. And there was no great flood of waters from that day forth.

THE STORY OF ABRAHAM AND ISAAC

Now one of the descendants of Noah was Abraham. Sarah, the wife of Abraham, bore him a son in his old age. And Sarah said, rejoicing, "God has made me to laugh so that all that hear me will laugh, for I have borne a son, Isaac, in my old age."

And it came to pass, when Isaac was well grown, that the Lord came unto Abraham and said, "Abraham, behold, here I am."

And He said, "Take now your only son, Isaac, whom you love, and get you into the land of Moriah. Slay Isaac and offer him there for a burnt offering upon one of the mountains which I will tell you of."

And Abraham rose up early in the morning and saddled his ass, and took two of his young men with him, and Isaac his son, and cut the wood for the burnt offering and went toward the place of which God had told him. Then on the third day, Abraham lifted up his eyes and saw the place afar off. And Abraham said unto the young men, "Abide ye here with the ass; and I and the lad will go yonder and worship and come again to you."

Abraham took the wood for the burnt offering, and laid it upon Isaac, his son. And Abraham took the fire in his hand, and a knife, and they went both of them together.

And Isaac spoke unto Abraham, his father, and said, "My father."

And Abraham answered, "Here am I, my son."

Isaac said, "My father, behold the fire and the wood, but where is the lamb for the burnt offering?"

And Abraham spoke, saying, "My son, God will provide Himself a lamb for the burnt offering." And they both went on together.

They came to the place of which God had told Abraham. And Abraham built an altar there and laid the wood in order, and bound Isaac his son. And Abraham stretched forth his hand, and he took the knife to slay his son for an offering even as the Lord had commanded.

And the angel of the Lord called unto him out of heaven and said, "Abraham, Abraham."

And Abraham answered, "Here am I."

And the angel said, "Lay not your hand upon the lad, neither do you anything unto him. For now I know you fear God, seeing you have not withheld your son, your only son, from me."

And Abraham lifted up his eyes and beheld a ram caught in a thicket by his horns. And Abraham went and took the ram and offered him up for a burnt offering instead of his son. And Abraham called the place Jehovah-jireh: as it is said to this day, "In the mount of the Lord it shall be seen."

JOSEPH AND
HIS BROTHERS

And it came to pass that when it was time for Isaac's son Jacob to marry, he went into the land of his father's people and took as his wife Rachel, the daughter of Laban. And Rachel bore him a son, who was called Joseph.

Joseph, being seventeen years old, tended his father's flocks with his brothers. But Jacob loved Joseph more than all his other children, and he made Joseph a coat of many colors. When the brothers saw that their father loved Joseph most, they hated Joseph.

Now Joseph dreamed a dream, and he told his brothers. He said unto them:

"Hear, I pray you, this dream which I have dreamed. For behold, we were binding sheaves of wheat in the field; and lo, my sheaf arose and stood upright, and your sheaves stood round about and bowed low before my sheaf."

His brothers said to him, "Shall you indeed reign over us, and shall you be ruler over us?" And they hated him yet more for his words.

Then Joseph dreamed yet another dream, and told his brothers: "Behold, the sun and the moon and eleven stars bowed before me."

And Joseph told the dream to his father also, and his father rebuked him, and said unto him, "What is this dream that you have dreamed? Shall I and your mother and your eleven brothers come to bow ourselves to earth before you?"

And Joseph's brothers were angry with the lad; but his father remembered the dream.

Now Joseph's brothers went to a distant place to feed their father's flocks. And Jacob said to Joseph, "I will send you unto your brothers. See whether it be well with them and with the flocks, and bring me word."

So Joseph went out from his father's house, and came near unto his brothers. And when they saw him afar off, they said one to another:

"Behold, this dreamer comes. Now, therefore, let us slay him and cast him into a pit, and we will say, 'An evil beast has devoured him, and we shall see what will become of his dreams."

And Joseph's brother Reuben heard it, and said, "Let us not kill him. Shed no blood, but cast him into this pit that is in the wilderness, and lay no hand upon him."

Reuben spoke thus so that he might take Joseph and bring him in safety to his father.

But when Reuben went away to tend his flock, the other brothers stripped Joseph of his coat of many colors, and they took him and cast him into an empty pit.

And they lifted up their eyes, and behold, a company of Ishmaelites came from the land of Gilead with their camels, bearing spices and balm and myrrh, carrying them down to Egypt. And one of the brothers, Judah, said:

"What gain is it if we leave our brother here to die? Come, let us sell him to the Ishmaelites, and let not our hand be upon him, for he is our brother and our flesh."

His brothers were content. They lifted Joseph out of the pit and sold him to the Ishmaelites for twenty pieces of silver. And the Ishmaelites brought Joseph into Egypt.

Now Reuben had been watching his flocks. When he came again to the pit and saw that Joseph was not there, he rent his clothes in wrath and terror. And he returned unto his brothers and said, "The child is gone; and I, whither shall I go?"

And his brothers took Joseph's coat and dipped it in the blood of a young goat they had killed. And they brought the coat of many colors to their father Jacob, and said, "This have we found. Say now whether or not this is your son's coat?"

Joseph's father knew it; and he said, "It is my son's coat; an evil beast has devoured him. He lives no more."

And Jacob rent his clothes, and wore sackcloth, and mourned for many days; nor would he be comforted.

And Jacob said, "I will go down into the grave mourning my son." Thus the father wept for his son Joseph.

Now when Joseph was brought down to Egypt, Potiphar, who was an officer of Pharaoh, King of Egypt, and captain of the guard, bought Joseph from the Ishmaelites. And the Lord was with Joseph, and Joseph found grace in the sight of his master Potiphar. And Potiphar made Joseph overseer in his house and over all he had.

Joseph was a goodly person and fair in the sight of men. But Potiphar's wife spoke evil words against Joseph, and he was cast into prison.

Even here the Lord was with Joseph and showed him mercy. For it came to pass that the butler of the King of Egypt had angered his master and he, also, was cast into prison. And the butler dreamed a dream, and Joseph said unto him, "Why do you look so sad?"

And the butler told his dream, saying:

"In my dream, behold, a vine was before me, and on the vine were three branches, and the vine budded; her blossoms shot forth; and the clusters brought forth ripe grapes. And Pharaoh's cup was in my hand, and I took the grapes and pressed them into Pharaoh's cup, and I gave the cup into Pharaoh's hand."

And Joseph said, "This is the meaning of it: Within three days shall Pharaoh send for you and restore you unto your place, and you shall again give Pharaoh his cup, and again you shall be his butler. But, I pray you, think of me when it is well with you. Speak of me unto Pharaoh. For, indeed, I have done nothing that they should put me into the dungeon."

It came to pass on the third day, which was Pharaoh's birthday, that Pharaoh made a feast unto all his servants. And he restored the chief butler to his place, and again the man gave to Pharaoh his cup. But in his happiness, he forgot Joseph, and the promise he had made in prison.

At the end of two full years, Pharaoh dreamed an evil dream. He called his butler to him and spoke:

"In my dream I beheld seven cows, fat and well-favored; they did feed in a meadow. And seven other cows came up after them, poor and lean. And the lean did eat up the seven fat cows; but when they had eaten, they were as ill-favored as in the beginning. And again I dreamed, and I saw seven ears of wheat come up on one stalk, full and good. And behold, seven ears that were withered, thin, and blasted sprang up after them. And the seven thin ears devoured and ate the seven good ears. Now, I told this dream unto the magicians, but none could tell me its meaning."

Then the chief butler related unto Pharaoh how Joseph had read his dream aright. And Pharaoh sent and called Joseph, and they brought him out of the dungeon.

35

When he had heard Pharoah's dream, he said: "The dreams of the Pharoah are one. The seven good cows are seven years, and the seven full ears of wheat are seven years; and the seven lean cows are seven years, and the seven blasted ears are seven years. What God is about to do, He shows unto Pharaoh. Behold, there shall come seven years of great plenty throughout all the land of Egypt; and there shall arise after them seven years of famine, and all the years of plenty shall be forgotten in the land of Egypt.

"Now, therefore, let the Pharaoh find a man both strong and wise, and let the Pharaoh place this man over all the land of Egypt; and let this man and the officers under him take up the fifth part of the grain in the land of Egypt in the good years. And let the food be kept for the years of famine, that the people of Egypt perish not."

Pharaoh heard these things, and he said unto his men, "Can we find another such man as this?" And he said to Joseph, "You shall be over my house, and over the people. Only I shall be greater than you."

Thus Pharaoh made Joseph ruler over all the land of Egypt. And Joseph went through the land of Egypt, telling the people that grain must be stored against the years of famine.

Now it came to pass after seven years that the great famine came in all countries. But there was food in Egypt for the people.

When Jacob the father of Joseph heard there was grain in Egypt, he sent Joseph's brothers to buy of it. Joseph was governor in the land, and sold grain to all the people that came thither. But Joseph's brothers knew him not, and they bowed themselves low before him.

Joseph knew his brothers, but made himself strange unto them. He commanded that their sacks be filled with grain, and that they be given food for their journey. And so they returned to their father Jacob.

A second time Jacob sent his sons to the land of Egypt. Joseph welcomed them to his house and gave them to eat and drink. And they took from their sacks presents they had brought—a little balm, a little honey, spices, myrrh, nuts, and almonds. But yet they knew Joseph not.

And Joseph's heart yearned over them; and after much time had passed, he made himself known unto them. And he wept aloud, and said: "I am Joseph; does my father yet live?"

His brothers could not answer him, for they were troubled and filled with fear.

And Joseph said, "Come here to me, I pray you." And they came near.

And Joseph said, "God has made me lord of all Egypt. Haste you and go to my father and tell him of my glory in Egypt, and you shall bring my father unto me."

And they went on their way and came
into the land of Canaan unto Jacob their father,
and told him, saying, "Joseph is yet alive, and
he is governor of all Egypt."

And Jacob's heart was faint, for he believed
them not. And they told him the words of
Joseph, and Jacob's spirit grew strong again.
And he said, "It is enough. Joseph, my son, is
yet alive. I will go and see him before I die."

And they took their cattle and their goods
and went into Egypt, Jacob and his sons, his
sons' sons with him; his daughters and his
sons' daughters. And he sent one unto Joseph
as a messenger. And Joseph made ready his
chariot and went to meet Jacob his father.

And Jacob said unto Joseph, "Now let me
die, since I have seen your face, because you
are yet alive."

And Jacob and Joseph's brothers dwelt with Joseph; and great was their prospering. And Jacob called his sons to him, and said, "Gather you together, that I may tell you what will befall you in the days that are to come."

And of Joseph, he spoke:

Joseph is a fruitful bough,
Even a fruitful bough by a well,
Whose branches run over the wall:
The archers have sorely grieved him,
And shot at him, and hated him:
But his bow abode in strength,
And the arms of his hands were made strong
By the hands of the mighty God of Jacob . . .
The blessings of the fathers have prevailed
Above the blessings of many generations
Unto the utmost bound of the everlasting hills;
They shall be upon the head of Joseph,
And on the crown of him that was separate
     from his brethren.

Thus did Jacob bless Joseph and praise him; for Jacob loved Joseph more than all his other children.

MOSES IN
THE BULRUSHES

Now the children of Jacob, who was also called Israel, and their children stayed in Egypt and multiplied and became mighty. But after many years, a new Pharaoh arose who remembered not Joseph's good deeds.

He hardened his heart against the children of Israel who dwelt in his lands. For he feared their strength and their numbers. Therefore Pharaoh set taskmasters over the Israelites to punish and burden them. They were made to build treasure cities, and to toil in the fields. And their days were bitter. Yet they grew ever stronger, and their numbers increased.

Then the Pharaoh sent forth a decree, saying, "Every man-child born of the people of Israel shall be slain, and every daughter saved alive."

Now there were in the land a man and a woman of the tribe of Joseph's brother Levi, who had a son born to them, a goodly child. And the mother in fear hid the child three months. And when she could no longer hide him, she made for him an ark of bulrushes, a cradle of reeds, and daubed it with pitch so that it would not sink. She put the child in it and laid it among the reeds and water lilies by the river bank. And the child's sister awaited far off to see what would be done.

Now the daughter of Pharaoh, proud and richly robed, came with her maidens to bathe in the river; and when she saw the ark among the reeds, she sent her maid to fetch it. When she opened it, she saw the child, and behold, the child wept. And she had pity on him, and said, "This is one of the Hebrew children."

Then the sister of the child drew near, and said to Pharaoh's daughter, "Shall I go and call to you a nurse from the Hebrew women, that she may care for the child?"

And Pharaoh's daughter said to her, "Go."

The child's sister went and called her mother. And Pharaoh's daughter said to her, "Take this child away and care for him, and I will bring you wages. And my word shall be a seal of safekeeping, both yours and the child's."

And the child's mother took him and cared for him.

Now the child grew, and when he had become a lad, the mother brought him again to Pharaoh's daughter. And Pharaoh's daughter said, "He shall be my son. And his name shall be called Moses, because I drew him out of the water."

And when Moses became a man he went among his brethren, the children of Israel, and looked on their burden. And the Lord appeared unto Moses out of the midst of a burning bush, saying:

"You shall lead My people out of the land of the Egyptian and bring them to a goodly land and large, a land flowing with milk and honey, even the land of Canaan."

And Moses said unto God, "Who am I, that I should go unto Pharaoh and that I should bring the children of Israel out of Egypt?"

And the Lord said, "Certainly I will be with you. And as a sign that I have chosen you, when you have brought the Hebrew people out of Egypt, you shall serve God upon the mountain."

And, as it was said that day, Moses was chosen by the Lord to lead the children of Israel out of the fields of bondage, free from the hand of Pharaoh.

CROSSING
THE RED SEA

And it came to pass that the Lord said unto
Moses, "You shall speak unto Pharaoh, that he
send the children of Israel out of his land."

Moses went to Pharaoh, and Pharaoh promised to let the Hebrews go free. But then
Pharaoh hardened his heart again, and would
not let the people go.

Now the Lord showed many signs and
wonders in the land of Egypt. He turned the
river of the Egyptians to blood and caused
frogs to come upon the land. He changed the
dust of the land, that it became lice; and sent a
swarm of flies into the house of Pharaoh and
into all the houses of Egypt. He brought death
to the cattle, the oxen, the asses, and the sheep
of the fields. But still Pharaoh would not let
the people go as he had promised Moses.

Then the Lord sent upon the Egyptians a plague of boils, and on the land there was hail, thunder, and fire.

Locusts covered the face of the earth, and not a green thing remained in the trees or in the herbs of the field.

A thick darkness fell upon the Egyptians; and they saw not one another nor rose from their dwellings for three days.

Still was Pharaoh's heart hardened, and he would not let the children of Israel depart from the land of Egypt.

And the Lord said unto Moses, "Yet will I bring one plague more upon Pharaoh. Afterward will he let you go hence."

And the Lord smote all the firstborn in the land of Egypt so that they died, from the firstborn of Pharaoh who sat upon his throne, even unto the firstborn of the maidservant in the mill and all the firstborn beasts. But the Lord passed over the houses of the children of Israel and did not suffer one to be destroyed.

And the Lord said unto Moses, "And it shall come to pass, when you are come to the land which the Lord will give you, that you shall make a service and a sacrifice, saying, 'It is the service of the Lord's passover, Who passed over the houses of the children of Israel in the land of Egypt, and harmed them not.' "

And it came to pass, when at midnight the Lord smote all the firstborn in the land of Egypt, that the Pharaoh rose up in the night. And he called for Moses, and said, "Rise up and go forth from among my people, both you and the children of Israel. Go serve the Lord."

47

The children of Israel went forth from the land of Egypt according to the word of Moses. And God led them through the wilderness by the Red Sea. He went before them by day in a pillar of cloud to lead them on the way, and by night in a pillar of fire to give them light.

Now it was told to Pharaoh that the people had fled. And the heart of Pharaoh and of his servants was turned against the people, and they said, "Why have we done this? Why have we let our servants, the people of Israel, go?"

And Pharaoh made ready his chariot, and took six hundred chosen chariots and all the chariots of Egypt, and captains over every one. And he followed after the children of Israel and overtook them where they were encamped by the sea. And when Pharaoh drew near, the children of Israel lifted up their eyes; and behold, the Egyptians marched after them.

Then the children of Israel were afraid, and cried out unto the Lord. And they said unto Moses, "Have you taken us away to die in the wilderness? Why did you lead us forth from the land of the Egyptians? Let us alone, that we may serve Pharaoh. For that is better than to die in the wilderness."

And Moses said, "Fear not, stand still and see what the Lord will show to you this day. The Lord will fight for you, and you shall hold your peace."

And the angel of God which went before the camp of Israel, now went behind; and the pillar of cloud went behind them. And it stood between the two camps. It was a cloud of darkness to the Egyptians, but it gave light by night to the children of Israel. And neither came near the other all night.

Now in the night Moses stretched out his hand over the sea, and the Lord caused the sea to go back. An east wind blew all night and made the sea dry land. And in the morning, the children of Israel went into the midst of the sea upon dry ground. And the waters were a wall on their right hand and on their left.

And the Egyptians rose and went in after them to the midst of the sea, even all Pharaoh's horses, his chariots, and his horsemen. And the Lord said unto Moses, "Stretch out your hand over the sea."

Moses stretched out his hand. And the waters returned and covered the chariots, the horsemen, and all the hosts of Pharaoh, so that they drowned. And not so much as one of them was left alive.

Thus the Lord saved Israel that day out of the hand of the Egyptians. Israel saw the great work of the Lord; and the people feared Him and believed the Lord and His servant Moses.

Then sang Moses and the children of Israel this song unto the Lord:

I will sing unto the Lord, for He hath triumphed gloriously.
The horse and his rider hath He thrown into the sea.
The Lord is my strength and song,
And he is become my salvation . . . .

The Lord is a man of war;
The Lord is His name.
Pharaoh's chariots and his hosts hath He cast into the sea:
His chosen captains also are drowned in the Red Sea.
The depths have covered them;
They sank to the bottom as a stone.

Who is like unto Thee, O Lord, among gods?
Who is like Thee, glorious in holiness,
Fearful in praises, doing wonders?
Thou stretchedst out Thy right hand,
The earth swallowed them.
Thou in mercy hast led forth the people which Thou hast saved;
Thou hast guided them in Thy strength unto Thy holy dwelling . . . .

The Lord shall reign for ever and ever.

And Miriam the prophetess, who was the sister of Moses, took a timbrel in her hand. She beat upon the small drum to make music; and all the women went out after her with timbrels, and they danced. And Miriam answered them:

Sing ye to the Lord, for He hath triumphed gloriously;
The horse and his rider hath He thrown into the sea.

THE TABLETS
OF STONE

In the third month after the children of Israel
were gone forth out of the land of Egypt, they
came into the wilderness of Sinai. They pitched
their tents in the desert at the foot of the mountain of Sinai. And Moses went up to the mount
unto God; and the Lord called unto him out of
the mountain, saying:

"Thus shall you tell the children of Israel:
'You have seen with what punishments I visited
the Egyptians and how I bore you, as on eagles'
wings, and brought you out of the land in safety.
Now, therefore, obey My voice, keep My covenant, and you shall be a treasure unto Me above
all people; for the earth is Mine.' "

And Moses went down from the mount unto
the people to prepare them for the word of the
Lord; and they washed their clothes. And he
said to them, "Be ready on the third day."

And it came to pass on the third day, in the morning, that there were thunders and lightnings, and a thick cloud upon the mount of Sinai. And the voice of the trumpet was exceeding loud, and the people trembled. And Moses brought the people forth from their camp to meet with God, and they stood at the foot of the mount. And Mount Sinai was covered with smoke because the Lord descended upon it in fire; and the smoke rose as from a furnace and the whole mountain shook greatly. And when the voice of the trumpet sounded long and grew louder, Moses spoke and the Lord answered him. And the Lord came down upon Mount Sinai, and He called upon Moses. And Moses went up to the top of the mountain.

And God spoke to Moses, saying, "I am the Lord your God, who has brought you out of the land of Egypt, out of the house of bondage. These are My laws. And I will show mercy unto the thousands who love Me and keep My commandments:

> *Thou shalt have no other gods before me.*
> *Thou shalt not bow thyself down to any graven image, or any likeness of any thing that is in the heaven above, or in the earth beneath, or in the water below the earth.*
> *Thou shalt not take the name of the Lord thy God in vain.*
> *Remember the Sabbath day, to keep it holy. Six days shalt thou labor, and do all thy work, but the seventh day is the Sabbath day of the Lord thy God. For in six days the Lord made heaven and earth, the sea and all that is in it; and rested the seventh day.*
> *Honor thy father and thy mother, that thy days may be long in the land which the Lord thy God giveth thee.*
> *Thou shalt not kill.*
> *Thou shalt not commit adultery.*
> *Thou shalt not steal.*
> *Thou shalt not speak falsely against thy neighbor.*
> *Thou shalt not covet thy neighbor's goods.*

And these are the Lord's ten commandments.

When the people saw the thunder and the lightning, and the mountain smoking, and when they heard the noise of the trumpet, they were afraid and stood back.

But Moses reassured them, and said to them, "Fear not." Then he went back into the thick darkness where God was.

The Lord spoke many other laws to Moses. And when He had finished speaking, He gave unto Moses two tablets of stone upon which were the words of the law, written with the finger of God.

And when Moses came down from the mountain with the tablets of stone in his hands, his face shone, though he knew it not.

When the children of Israel saw Moses, and beheld that his face shone, they were afraid to come near him. And Moses called unto the rulers of the people, and they answered him; and Moses talked with them. And then all the children of Isarel came near; and Moses gave them the laws and commandments which the Lord had spoken to him on Mount Sinai.

THE GOLDEN CALF

Now while Moses was upon Mount Sinai, Aaron the brother of Moses became the leader of the children of Israel. The people gathered themselves together and said unto him, "Make us gods, which shall go before us. As for this Moses, the man that brought us up out of the land of Egypt, we know not what is become of him. He has not returned unto us."

And Aaron said unto them, "Break off the golden earrings which are in the ears of your wives, of your sons, of your daughters, and bring them unto me."

And all the people broke the golden earrings which were in their ears and brought them unto Aaron. And he melted them and made a golden calf, and fashioned it with a graving tool. And they said, "These be the gods, O Israel, which brought you out of the land of Egypt."

Aaron built an altar before the golden calf. And he made a proclamation, and said, "To-morrow is a feast of the Lord."

And the people rose up early and offered burnt offerings; and they sat down to eat and drink, and rose up to play. Greatly did they rejoice.

On Mount Sinai, the voice of the Lord said to Moses, "Get you down off the mountain; for your people have turned aside out of the way I commanded them. They have made a golden calf and worshiped it. My wrath has waxed hot against them. Go you into the Promised Land whither you are journeying, a land flowing with milk and honey. But I will not go with you or with your people lest, in My anger, I utterly consume them."

Moses went down from Mount Sinai. And a man came to him, saying, "There is a noise of war in the camp."

And Moses answered, "It is not the voice of those that shout for victory nor is it the voice of those that cry because they are overcome, but the noise of singing that I hear."

And when Moses saw the calf and the
dancing, his wrath was very great. He took the
calf which they had made and burned it in the
fire and ground it to powder and strewed it
upon the water and made the children of Israel
drink of it.

And Moses said, "You have sinned a great sin. The Lord has turned His face from you; He will surely destroy you. He will not be with you in the Promised Land, but will blot you out of His book so that not one of you remains."

The people mourned, for they feared the Lord would consume them, even unto the women and children.

When Moses heard their cries, he took the tabernacle of the Lord and pitched it far from the camp. And those that sought the Lord followed Moses. They rose up, and every man stood at his tent door and looked after him.

And it came to pass, as Moses entered into the tabernacle, that the cloudy pillar descended and stood at the door; and the Lord talked to Moses, face to face, as a man speaks unto his friend.

And Moses said unto the Lord, "Now, therefore, I pray You declare the way that I may find grace in Your sight; and consider that this nation is Your people. And I beseech You, show me Your glory."

And the Lord said, "My presence shall go with you, and I will give you rest. I will make all My goodness pass before you, and proclaim the name of the Lord before you."

Then Moses turned again to the children of Israel. When they saw him, they knew the Lord was with them and with Moses, who had brought them forth out of the land of Egypt.

DAVID AND GOLIATH

It came to pass that when the children of Israel reached the land promised to them by the Lord, and conquered the peoples in it, the land was divided by lot among the nine tribes of Israel. A certain piece of land was given to the children of Judah, Joseph's brother. They settled on the land, and prospered, and after many years the land itself came to be called Judah.

In the days when Saul was King of Israel, there lived near the city of Bethlehem in Judah, Jesse, a godly man, and his eight sons. He was grown old and burdened with years. His three oldest sons, Eliab, Abinadab, and Shammah, had followed Saul into battle. But the youngest son, David, kept his father's sheep.

Now the Philistines, who were enemies of the Hebrews, were camped on one side of the mountains, seeking to destroy Israel. On the other side, with the valley between them, were the armed hosts of Israel. And the two armies prepared for battle.

Now there went out from the camp of the Philistines a champion, Goliath of Gath. He was tall as a man and half as tall again. He wore on his head a helmet of brass; he was clothed with heavy armor; greaves of brass were on his legs, and a shield of brass between his shoulders. The staff of his spear was heavy, and his spear's head weighed six hundred shekels of iron.

When Goliath stood in the sun, he was like a tower of brass, and the brightness of his armor struck the hearts of the men of Israel with fear.

His voice was like a trumpet of brass as he called out across the valley of peril:

"Choose you a man for your people. Let him come down to me. If he is able to fight with me and kill me then we, the Philistines, will be your servants. But if I prevail against him, then you shall be our servants, you and your children all the years of your life."

For forty days, morning and evening, Goliath strode between the two armies. But no one in all Israel stepped forth to do battle with him.

Now it came to pass that at evening, when his sheep were safe in the fold, David went to the house of Jesse his father. And Jesse spoke to him, saying:

"Take a measure of this parched corn and these ten loaves, and carry them to your brothers. Take also these ten cheeses to the captain of the men with whom your brothers are encamped. Look, and see well how it fares with your brothers."

David rose early in the morning and left the sheep with a keeper. When he came to the vale of Elah, where the men of Israel were, he left all that he had brought with the keeper of the King's goods. And he hastened forward into the valley, where Saul's army was already in battle.

And David saw Goliath the champion, and heard his voice echoing among the hills:

"Send you a man who will dare to come down and do battle with me."

The men of Israel fled before Goliath, and were sore afraid. And they said to David:

"Have you not seen this giant Goliath? Have you not heard his words?"

And David answered them: "Yea, forty days, morning and evening, have I heard him." And he asked, "What will be the reward of the man who kills this Philistine? Who is this Goliath of Gath that he defies the armies of the living God?"

The people answered, "The King will give him who slays the giant great riches; and the King will give him his daughter, and will make his father's house free in Israel."

Of many David asked the question, and always they answered the same. But Eliab, his eldest brother, heard how David spoke to the men, and was angry.

"Why have you, a stripling, come down among the men of battle, and why do you walk among the tents of them that fight?"

"Did I not bring food, and was not the reason of my coming good?" answered David.

"With whom did you leave the sheep? In the wilderness did you leave them?"

David spoke again, "A guard I set over them in my father's pasture. What then have I done wrong?"

Eliab shouted in his wrath: "I know your pride and the wickedness of your heart. You have come to see the battle."

David turned away from Eliab, and again asked of all he met, "What shall be the gift to him who takes this curse from Israel?"

66

Now those that heard David speak brought word of him to Saul the King. Saul knew David and sent for him, and he looked with joy on the young shepherd. For the lad was like a prince, though he stood before the leader of Israel clad only in his simple herdsman's tunic, a leather belt at his waist, from which hung a bag for his sling and stones. On his feet were leather sandals.

And David said to the King:

"Let no man's heart know fear because of this Goliath come out of Gath, for I thy servant will go and fight with him."

Saul answered David. "You cannot go against this Philistine to fight him. You are but a youth, and he a man of war."

And David said, "I thy servant keep my father's sheep; and when a lion and a bear came and took a lamb out of the flock, I went out after them. I smote them and took the lamb out of their mouths. I caught them by the head and slew them. I slew both the lion and the bear, so will I smite this Philistine who stands against the armies of Israel."

Saul then answered, "A mighty man and a man of strength is this Goliath." And David said, "The Lord delivered me out of the paw of the lion and out of the paw of the bear; He will deliver me from the hand of the Philistine."

Saul gave to David his blessing, saying, "Go, and the Lord shall be with you."

And Saul put on David his own helmet of brass and his armor and gave to David his sword. But David said to Saul, "I cannot go forth with these, for I have not worn nor tried them."

And David put them from him, and took his staff in his hand. He knelt by the brook and chose five smooth stones, and put them in his shepherd's bag. His sling was in his hand. And David drew near the Philistine.

When the giant saw David he despised him. For he was but a youth, ruddy, and with a fair, open countenance. And Goliath called to David in a voice of wrath.

"Am I then a dog that you come against me with but a staff in your hand?"

The Philistine raised his sword. It was as tall as David. "Come to me," cried the giant, "and I will give your bones to the birds of the air and the beasts of the field."

Then David said to the Philistine, "You stand before me with a sword, a spear, and a javelin. But I come to you in the name of the Lord of hosts, God of the armies of Israel. The battle is the Lord's."

David moved close and spoke again.

"This day the Lord will deliver you into my hand. I will smite you, and your head from you. I will give the bones of the host of the Philistine to the wild beasts of the earth and the birds of the air. The earth will know there is a God in Israel."

The Philistine went down toward David, and David ran toward the army of the enemy to meet him.

David took a stone from his bag and sent it straight from his sling. The stone struck Goliath in the forehead, and the giant fell upon his face, dead. Then David ran and stood over the Philistine and took his sword and cut off his head with its broad blade.

When the Philistines saw that their champion was dead, they fled; and the men of Israel rose and drove them far from the land.

David took the head of Goliath to Jerusalem, the King's city, and gave it to the King. And as he passed along the way, women came from all the cities of Israel, singing and dancing. With timbrels they sang joyfully:

 *Saul has slain his thousands and David his ten thousands.*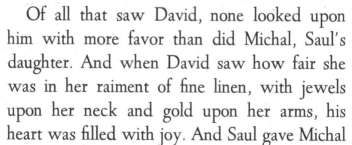

Of all that saw David, none looked upon him with more favor than did Michal, Saul's daughter. And when David saw how fair she was in her raiment of fine linen, with jewels upon her neck and gold upon her arms, his heart was filled with joy. And Saul gave Michal to David for his wife.

And from that day forth, Michal greatly loved the young shepherd come out of Bethlehem of Judah. And Saul the King knew that the Lord was with David.

THE
TWENTY-THIRD PSALM

Now Saul took David into his house and would not let him return to his father. David played the harp in the presence of King Saul and sang songs, which are called Psalms. And this is one of David's psalms:

The Lord is my shepherd; I shall not want.
He maketh me to lie down in green pastures;
He leadeth me beside the still waters.
He restoreth my soul;
He leadeth me in the paths of righteousness for
    His name's sake.
Yea, though I walk through the valley of the shadow
    of death,
I will fear no evil; for Thou art with me;
Thy rod and Thy staff they comfort me.
Thou preparest a table before me in the presence of
    mine enemies:
Thou anointest my head with oil; my cup runneth over.
Surely goodness and mercy shall follow me all the
    days of my life,
And I will dwell in the house af the Lord forever.

DANIEL IN
THE LION'S DEN

It came to pass that the kingdom of Judah fell
under the rule of the Medes, a strong, warlike
nation. And in the days when Darius the
Mede ruled in the land, he placed over it a hundred and twenty princes. Of these the first was
Daniel, a Hebrew captive from the kingdom
of Judah. Daniel was chosen above all in Israel
because an excellent spirit was in him. And
Darius thought to set him over the whole realm.

It came to pass that the rulers and governors
who were less favored than Daniel were
angered, and sought to bring him down from
his high place. But they found no fault in him.
Then said these men: "We can prove no wrong
against Daniel, except we find it in the law by
which he worships the God of Israel."

And the rulers and governors went before the King, and said thus to him:

"King Darius, live forever. All the governors and the rulers, the wise and the mighty, have gathered together to make a decree that whosoever shall pray to any god or man for thirty days, save only you, O King, that one shall be thrown into a den of lions. Now make firm this rule, O King, and sign the writing that it be not changed, according to the law of the Medes and the Persians, which alters not."

Wherefore King Darius signed the writing and the decree.

Daniel knew the writing was signed. But he went into his house; and his window being open in his chamber, he went down on his knees three times a day, and prayed and gave thanks to his God as he had before. And Daniel knew in his heart how great is the word of the Lord, and mightier than the laws of kings.

Those who had appeared before Darius came together and found Daniel praying unto his God. Then they returned to the King, and spoke before the King concerning his decree:

"Have you not signed a decree that whosoever, for thirty days, shall pray to his god or ask anything of any man save only you, O King, that one shall be cast into a den of lions?"

The King answered and said, "The thing is true, according to the law of the Medes and the Persians, which alters not."

Then answered they, and said before the King, "That Daniel, a captive of the kingdom of Judah, obeys not the King; but three times a day, prays before his God."

When the King heard these words, he was sore displeased with himself, and set his heart on Daniel to deliver him; and he labored till the going down of the sun to save him. Then the rulers and governors came to the King, and said, "Know, O King, that the law of the Medes and Persians is that no decree which the King makes may be changed."

Then the King commanded, and they brought Daniel. And the King said to Daniel:

"Your God, whom you continually serve, He will deliver and save you."

Now stone was brought and laid upon the mouth of the lions' den; and the King sealed it with his own signet, and with the signet of the lords. This he did, that all might know that the thing had been done by decree of the King and might not be changed.

Then Darius went to his palace and passed the night fasting; nor was any music played before him. His sleep went from him, and he rested not.

The King arose very early in the morning, and went in haste unto the den of lions. And when he came to the den, he cried loudly unto Daniel and said, "O Daniel, servant of the living God, is that God whom you continually serve able to save you from the lions?"

Then said Daniel unto the King, "O King, live forever. My God has sent His angel and has shut the lions' mouths, so that they have not hurt me: for no wrong was found in me before the Lord; and also before you, O King, have I done no hurt."

Then was the King exceedingly glad for him, and commanded that Daniel should be taken up out of the den. And no hurt was found upon him, because he believed in his God.

And the King commanded, and they brought those men which had accused Daniel, and cast them, and their wives and their children, into the den of lions; and the lions broke all their bones in pieces before they came to the bottom of the den.

Then King Darius wrote unto all people, nations, and languages that dwelt in all the earth:

"Peace be unto you. I make a decree: that in every dominion of my kingdom men tremble and fear before the God of Daniel: for He is the living God, and steadfast forever, and His kingdom is that which shall not be destroyed, and His dominion shall be even unto the end. He delivers and rescues, and He works signs and wonders in heaven, who has delivered Daniel from the power of the lions."

So Daniel prospered in the reign of Darius, and in the reign of Cyrus the Persian, who came after Darius.

JONAH
AND THE WHALE

About the time of Daniel, the Lord spoke to
his prophet Jonah, saying, "Arise, go to Nineveh,
that wicked city of the Babylonians, and cry
against its evil and the sins of its people, lest
they be destroyed."

Jonah heard the voice of the Lord, but fled
from him and went down to the shore of the
Mediterranean. There he found a ship going to
Tarshish, a foreign city. He paid his fare and
set forth to hide from the Lord.

But the Lord sent a mighty tempest; the skies were black as night, yet no stars shone. The waves rose higher than the ship's mast; the sound of the wind was a cry of wrath. Now the ship lay on one side, now on the other. The waves were above it like mountains, and the boat was about to be broken. Every mariner was sore afraid, and each man cried unto his God. They cast all their goods from the ship to lighten it.

Jonah was inside the ship, and he lay fast asleep. The shipmaster came to Jonah, and said: "Arise, O sleeper, and call upon your God; pray to Him that we perish not!"

Then the mariners spoke to one another: "One among us has brought this evil on the ship. Let us draw lots that we may find him."

And the lot fell upon Jonah. And they asked him, "Tell us, we pray, from what country do you come and of what people are you?"

And Jonah answered, "I am a Hebrew, and I fear the Lord Who made the sea and the dry land."

Now the men trembled. They knew Jonah had fled from the Lord, for he had told them.

They said unto him: "What shall we do unto you, so that the sea shall be calm for us?"

For the waves rose ever higher, and the ship lay on her side as if to sink beneath them, and the mast was split in two.

Jonah answered them, "Take me up, cast me forth into the sea. Then shall the waves be calm. For my sake, because I fled from the Lord, the great tempest is upon you."

The mariners rowed hard to bring the ship to land, but they could not. And they prayed to their God, saying, "Let us not perish for this man's life, O Lord. Yet lay not the death of an innocent man upon us. For, O Lord, You have done as You so willed."

Then they took Jonah up and cast him into the sea. And the sea was calm.

Now the Lord had prepared a great fish, which swallowed Jonah. And Jonah was in the fish three days and three nights. And Jonah prayed to God from the belly of the fish:

I cried by reason of mine affliction unto the Lord,
And He heard me....
All Thy billows and Thy waves passed over me.
Then I said, "I am cast out of Thy sight;
Yet I will look again toward Thy holy temple."
The waters compassed me about, even to the soul:
The depths closed me round about,
The weeds were wrapped about my head.
I went down to the bottoms of the mountains...
When my soul fainted within me I remembered
*   the Lord; and my prayer came in unto Thee.*
Yet hast Thou brought up my life from corruption,
*   O Lord my God....*
I will sacrifice unto Thee with the voice of thanks-
*   giving;*
I will pay that I have vowed
Salvation is of the Lord.

Then the Lord spoke unto the fish, and the fish opened his great gaping mouth and cast Jonah forth upon the dry land.

And the Lord said again to Jonah, "Arise, go unto Nineveh, and preach unto it the words I bid you."

So Jonah rose and went to Nineveh. He went through its streets, where men walked in rich garments, and beggars knelt faint with hunger, where women gleamed with jewels and others wept in rags. He went about the city and cried out as the Lord had told him:

"In forty days Nineveh shall be overthrown. Because of its sins will it perish."

The people of Nineveh believed God and His prophet, Jonah, and they proclaimed a fast and put on sackcloth, from the greatest of them unto the least. Word came unto the King of Nineveh, and he arose from his golden throne; he laid his jeweled robes aside and covered himself with sackcloth, and as a sign that he and his people repented, he sat down among the ashes. And he caused it to be proclaimed:

"Let neither men nor beast, herd nor flock, taste anything; let every man be covered with sackcloth, even with ashes. Let each one turn from his evil way and from violence. So may it be that God will see and repent and turn His wrath from us and His fierce anger."

And God saw their works, that they turned from their evil way; and God repented of the evil that He had said He would do unto them; and he did it not.

Jonah left the walls of Nineveh and went to the east of the city. He built himself an arbor and sat beneath it, waiting to see what would befall the city. Jonah watched for its towers and palaces to fall into dust before the anger of the Lord.

Long he looked, yet nothing stirred save a flock of birds going out to the grain fields. Jonah was filled with wrath that the Lord had not destroyed the people of Nineveh. The city still stood, unworthy of God's favor, a place of strangers.

And God spoke to Jonah: "Is it right that you are angry?"

And Jonah answered: "It is right. It is because of this that I fled from Your sight unto Tarshish. For I knew You to be merciful even to the strangers, they that are the people of Nineveh. I said in my heart, 'And if the Lord spare this place, why then shall I cry out against it?' Wherefore now, O Lord, take my life from me."

And the Lord prepared a gourd and made it to come up over Jonah, that it might be a shadow over his head, to deliver him from his grief. And Jonah was exceedingly glad of the gourd.

And when the morning rose the next day, God prepared a worm, and it caused the gourd to wither.

And it came to pass when the sun rose, that God sent an east wind; and the sun beat upon the head of Jonah, that he grew faint and said, "It is better for me to die than to live."

And God said to Jonah, "Art thou right to be angry for the gourd?"

And he said: "I do well to be angry, even unto death."

The Lord said, "In your heart was pity for this gourd when it withered away. Yet you did not plant it, nor water it, nor tend it as it grew. How much more shall I, the Lord, have pity on these people, who know not their right hand from their left? And should I not spare Nineveh, that great city, its men and its cattle? I, your God, will show mercy toward the strangers in a distant land. And salvation is to them in a far country, even as to Mine own people, those that dwell in Israel."

THE STORY OF ESTHER

Now it came to pass than when King Ahasuerus sat on the throne of Persia, he chose from among the maidens of many lands the beautiful maiden Esther. Mordecai the Jew had brought her up as his daughter, for she had no father or mother. Mordecai charged Esther, when she went into Shushan, the palace, that she tell not of her father or her kindred. And Esther did as Mordecai commanded.

The King loved Esther above all women. He set the royal crown upon her head and made her his Queen. Then the King made a great feast, a feast for Esther, and he rejoiced and gave gifts.

And in those days, Mordecai was a guard at the King's gate.

Now two of the King's chamberlains were angry, and sought to lay hands upon the King to harm him. When the thing became known to Mordecai, he told Esther. And in Mordecai's name, Esther gave warnings to the King. The two chamberlains were hanged in a tree; and it was written in the book of the chronicles for King Ahasuerus.

After these happenings, the King did promote Haman, another chamberlain, and set him
above all other princes. The King's servants
that were at the King's gate bowed before Haman, but Mordecai the Jew did not bow. Then
was Haman full of wrath. But he scorned to lay
hands on Mordecai alone. He sought to destroy
with him all the Jews in the land.

Haman sent letters sealed with the King's
seal throughout the land. In them it was ordered
that all Jews, both young and old, the little
children and the women, be slain in one day.
In every part of the land there was great mourning among the Jews, and fasting and weeping
and wailing.

And Haman had a great gallows built on
which to hang Mordecai.

Mordecai sent word to Esther: "Go you
before the King and ask mercy for your people.
Think not that you shall escape in the King's
palace more than all Jews. If you hold your
peace at this time, you and your father's house
shall be destroyed."

Now Esther was in great fear of the King,
but she bade a messenger say to Mordecai, "I
and my maidens will fast. Then I will go before
the King, And if I perish, I perish."

Esther put on her royal apparel and stood in the inner court of the King's house. And the King received her.

Esther said, "If I have found favor in your sight, O King, let my life be given me and the life of my people. For we are sold, I and my people, to be destroyed, to be slain, and to perish."

And the King answered, "Who is he and where is he, that plots in his heart to do so?"

And Esther answered, "The enemy is the wicked Haman." And when the King knew it was Haman who had done this thing, he had him hanged on the gallows, even on the gallows Haman had built for Mordecai the Jew.

And Mordecai was set in the place of Haman. And Mordecai sent letters in the King's name, and sealed with the King's seal, wherein it was written that the Jews henceforth should know neither harm nor fear. And in every province in every city wheresoever the King's decree came, the Jews had joy and gladness and a good day.

It was commanded that the Jews keep each
year a feast in memory of the day and the
month wherein they were saved by Esther the
Queen. These days were called the feast of
Purim, and were to be remembered and kept
throughout every generation, every family, every
province, and every city.

A PROPHECY

The house of Jesse, father of King David, the children of it and their generation, were like a great tree from which was to come marvelous fruit, like a shepherd's staff, suddenly blossoming. From the house of Jesse and the house of David was to come a Messiah, the anointed one, the Saviour.

In ancient days the Prophet Isaiah sang:

And there shall come forth a rod out of the stem
of Jesse,
And a Branch shall grow out of his roots.

And the spirit of the Lord shall rest upon him,
The spirit of wisdom and understanding,
The spirit of counsel and might,
The spirit of knowledge and of the fear of the Lord.

And Isaiah spoke:

The people that walked in darkness
Have seen a great light.
They that dwell in the land of the shadow of death,
Upon them hath the light shined.
For unto us a child is born, and unto us a son is given;
And His name shall be called
Wonderful, Counsellor, the mighty God,
The everlasting Father, the Prince of Peace,
From henceforth, even forever.

Thus did Isaiah foretell the coming of Jesus of Nazareth. But before Jesus' time were yet many prophets, and the last of these was John, the son of Zacharias and his wife Elizabeth.

THE NEW TESTAMENT

JOHN THE BAPTIST

When the time grew near that the words of the prophet Isaiah were to be fulfilled, a son was born to Elizabeth and Zacharias. And he was called John, as it was foretold by an angel of the Lord.

And the hand of the Lord was with John. And his father Zacharias was filled with the spirit of God, and prophesied, saying:

> Blessed be the Lord God of Israel;
> For He hath visited and redeemed His people.
> And thou, child, shalt be called the prophet of
>   the Highest;
> For thou shalt go before the face of the Lord to
>   prepare His ways;
> To give knowledge of salvation unto his people,
> Through the tender mercy of our God . . .
> To give light to them that sit in darkness
>   and the shadow of death,
> To guide our feet into the way of peace.

And the child John grew and waxed strong in spirit. And he dwelt in the desert, and was clothed with camels' hair and with a girdle of skin; and he did eat locusts and wild honey.

John baptized people in the wilderness. And there went out unto him all the land of Judea, and they of Jerusalem, and were baptized by him in the river Jordan, confessing their sins. And John preached, saying:

"There shall come one mightier than I, the thongs of whose shoes I am not worthy to stoop down and unloose. I indeed have baptized you with water; but He shall baptize you with the spirit of God."

So was the voice of the prophets fulfilled:

Behold, I shall send my messenger before Thy face,
Which shall prepare Thy way before Thee.
The voice of one crying in the wilderness,
"Prepare ye the way of the Lord,
Make His paths straight."

JESUS IS BORN

In the days of Caesar Augustus, ruler of the Romans and of all lands, the time came of which the prophets spoke.

The angel Gabriel was sent from God unto the city of Nazareth, to a maiden promised in marriage to a man whose name was Joseph, of the house of David. The maiden's name was Mary. And the angel came unto her and said: "Hail thou that are highly favored, the Lord is with thee; blessed art thou among women."

And when Mary saw him, she was troubled. And the angel said: "Fear not, Mary, for you have found favor with God. Behold, you shall bear a son and shall call him Jesus. He shall be great and shall be called the Son of the Highest; and the Lord God shall give to Him the throne of His father David; and He shall reign forever; and of His kingdom there shall be no end."

And Mary said, "Behold the handmaid of the Lord, be it according to thy word."

And the angel departed, and Mary spoke:

My soul doth magnify the Lord,
And my spirit hath rejoiced in God my Savior.
For He hath regarded the low estate of His
*   hand-maiden.*
For, behold, from henceforth all generations
*   shall call me blessed.*

Now it came to pass in those days that Caesar Augustus decreed that a census should be taken of all the world.

All the people went to be counted, every one into his own city. And Joseph, with Mary his wife, also went up from the land of Galilee into Judea, unto the city of David which is called Bethlehem, to be taxed. And while they were there, Mary brought forth her first-born son and wrapped Him in swaddling clothes, and laid Him in a manger; because there was no room for them in the inn.

And there were in that same country shepherds abiding in the field, keeping watch over their flock by night. And lo, the angel of the Lord came upon them, and the glory of the Lord shone round about them; and they were sore afraid. And the angel said unto them:

"Fear not: for behold, I bring you good tidings of great joy, which shall be to all people. For unto you is born this day, in the city of David, a Saviour, which is Christ the Lord. And you shall find the babe wrapped in swaddling clothes, lying in a manger."

And suddenly there was with the angel a multitude of the heavenly host praising God, and saying: "Glory to God in the highest, and on earth peace, good will toward men."

And it came to pass, as the angels were gone away into Heaven, that the shepherds said one to another: "Let us now go unto Bethlehem, and see this thing which is come to pass, which the Lord has made known unto us."

And they came with haste and found Mary and Joseph, and the babe lying in a manger. And when they had seen it, they made it known among the people, saying what was told them concerning the child. And all that heard it wondered at those things which were told them by the shepherds. But Mary kept all these things and pondered them in her heart. And the shepherds returned, glorifying and praising God for all the things they had heard and seen, as it was told unto them.

Now Jesus was born in Bethlehem of Judea, in the days when Herod was King of that country. And behold, there came wise men from the east, saying: "Where is He that is born King of the Jews? For we have seen His star in the east, and are come to worship Him."

When Herod heard these things, he was troubled, for he feared a new leader of the people. And he gathered the chief priests and the leaders of the land together and demanded that they tell him where Christ would be born.

And they said unto him, "In Bethlehem of Judea: for thus is it written by the prophet."

Now Herod had secretely called the wise men. And he sent them to Bethlehem, and said, "Go and search for the young child; and when you have found Him, bring me word, that I may come and worship Him also."

When they had heard the King, the wise men departed; and lo, the star which they had seen in the east went before them, till it came and stood over where the young child was. When they saw the star, they rejoiced with exceeding great joy. And when they came into the house, they saw the young child with Mary His mother, and fell down and worshiped Him. And they presented unto Him gifts: gold, and frankincense, and myrrh.

Now God warned the wise men in a dream that they should not return unto Herod, lest he ask them about the child and bring harm upon Him. The wise men therefore departed into their own country by another way.

As it is written in the law of the Lord, when some days had passed, Joseph and Mary took the child Jesus to Jerusalem to present Him to God in the temple and to offer a sacrifice, a pair of turtle doves and two young pigeons.

And behold, there was a man in Jerusalem whose name was Simeon; and the man was just and devout, waiting for the hope of Israel. And the spirit of God was upon him, and the spirit of God had shown unto him that he should not see death before he had seen the Lord's Christ. And the spirit led him into the temple. And when the parents brought in the Child Jesus, then Simeon took Him up into his arms, and said:

> Lord, lettest Thou Thy servant depart in peace.
> According to Thy word:
> For mine eyes have seen Thy salvation,
> Which Thou hast prepared before the face of all
>   people:
> A light to lighten the Gentiles,
> And the glory of Thy people Israel.

And Joseph and His mother marveled at those things which were spoken of the child, and Simeon prophesied concerning Him, and he blessed them.

FLIGHT INTO EGYPT

Now behold, the angel of the Lord appeared to Joseph in a dream, saying:

"Arise and take the young child and His mother, and flee into Egypt, and remain there until I bring you word. For Herod the King will seek the young child to destroy Him."

Joseph arose and took the young child and His mother by night, and departed into Egypt and was there until the death of Herod, that it might be fulfilled which was spoken of the Lord by the prophet, saying, "Out of Egypt have I called My Son."

But when Herod was dead, behold, an angel of the Lord appeared in a dream to Joseph in Egypt, saying: "Arise, and take the young child and His mother and go into the land of Israel; for they are dead which sought the young child's life."

And Joseph arose and took the young child and His mother, and came into the land of Israel. And he came and dwelt in a city called Nazareth, that it might be fulfilled which was spoken of the Saviour by the prophets: "He shall be called a Nazarene."

And when they had returned unto Galilee, to the city of Nazareth, the child grew and waxed strong in spirit, and the grace of God was upon Him.

THE BOY JESUS IN
THE TEMPLE

Now the parents of Jesus went to Jerusalem
every year at the Feast of the Passover. And
when He was twelve years old, they went up
to Jerusalem, after the custom of the feast. When
they had fulfilled the days, as they returned,
the child tarried behind them in Jerusalem; and
Joseph and Mary knew not of it. But they,
supposing Him to have been in the company,
went a day's journey; and they sought Him
among their kinsfolk and acquaintances. And
when they found Him not, they turned back
again to Jerusalem, seeking Him.

And it came to pass that after three days,
they found Him in the temple, sitting in the
midst of the rabbis, the teachers of the people,
both hearing them and asking questions. And
all that heard Him were astonished at His understanding and answers.

And when Joseph and Mary saw Him, they were amazed, and His mother said unto Him, "Son, why have You thus dealt with us? Behold, Your father and I have sought You, sorrowing."

And He said unto them, "How is it that you sought Me? Know you not that I must be about My Father's business?"

And they understood not the saying which He spoke unto them. And He went down with them and came to Nazareth, and was obedient unto them. But His mother kept all these sayings in her heart.

And Jesus the boy grew, and increased in wisdom and stature, and in favor with God and man.

JESUS AND
HIS DISCIPLES

And when Jesus was about thirty years of age,
He came from Nazareth of Galilee. And by the
river Jordan was John, son of Zacharias and of
Elizabeth. He was preaching the word of the
Lord as it is written by the prophet Isaiah:.

> The voice of one crying in the wilderness,
> "Prepare ye the way of the Lord,
> Make His paths straight."
> And every valley shall be filled,
> And every mountain and hill shall be brought low;
> And the crooked shall be made straight,
> And the rough ways shall be made smooth,
> And all men shall see the salvation of God.

And Jesus was baptized by John in the river
Jordan. And there came a voice from Heaven,
saying, "Thou art My beloved Son in Whom I
am well pleased."

And the Spirit of God drove Jesus into the wilderness. And He was there in the wilderness forty days and forty nights. And the devil tempted Him. But Jesus said unto him, "Thou shalt not tempt the Lord thy God." And the devil departed from Him.

Then came Jesus into Galilee preaching the gospel, the good news, saying, "The time is fulfilled and the kingdom of God is at hand."

It came to pass, that as people pressed upon Him to hear the word of God, He stood by the lake of Gennesaret. And He saw two ships standing out by the lake, but the fishermen were gone out of them and were washing their nets. And He entered into one of the ships which belonged to the fisherman Simon, whom Jesus called Peter, and prayed that he would go out a little from the land. And He taught the people from the ship.

And when He had finished speaking, He said unto Simon Peter, "Launch out into the deep and let down your nets for a draught."

Simon Peter, answering, said unto Him, "Master, we have toiled all the night and have taken nothing. Nevertheless, at Thy word, I will let down the net."

And when they had done this, they caught such a multitude of fishes that their nets became heavy and broke. And they beckoned to their partners who were in the other ship, that they should come and help them. And they came and filled both ships so full that they began to sink.

When Simon Peter saw it, he fell down at the knees of Jesus, saying, "Depart from me; for I am a sinful man, O Lord."

For he and all that were with him were astonished at the draught of fishes which they had taken.

And so also were James and John, the sons of Zebedee who were partners with Simon Peter.

And Jesus said unto Peter, "Fear not; from henceforth you shall be fishers of men; you shall be My Apostles."

And when they had brought their ships to land, they forsook all and followed Him. So also did others, up to the number of twelve, who became His Apostles. And the multitude gathered round about Him, and He taught them.

And behold, a certain lawyer stood up, saying, "Master, what shall I do to inherit eternal life?"

Jesus replied, "How read you the law?"

And the man answered Him, and said, "'Thou shalt love the Lord thy God with all thy heart, and with all thy soul, and with all thy strength, and with all thy mind, and thy neighbor as thyself.'"

And Jesus said, "This do, and you shall live."

But the lawyer asked again, "And who is my neighbor?"

And Jesus, answering, said: "A certain man went down from Jerusalem to Jericho, and fell among thieves, who stripped him of his robes and wounded him, and departed, leaving him half dead. And by chance there came down a certain priest that way; and when he saw him, he passed by on the other side.

"And likewise, a man of the tribe of Levi, when he was at the place, came and looked on him, and passed by on the other side.

"But a certain Samaritan, as he journeyed, came where the man was, and when he saw him, he had compassion on him, and went to him, and bound up his wounds, pouring in oil and wine, and set him on his own beast, and brought him to an inn, and took care of him. And in the morning when he departed, he took out two pence, and gave them to the innkeeper, and said unto him, 'Take care of him; and whatsoever more you spend, when I come again, I will repay you.'

"Which now of these three, think you, was the neighbor unto him that fell among thieves?"

And the lawyer answered, "He that showed mercy on him."

Then said Jesus unto him, "Go, and do you likewise."

And Jesus' disciples pondered in their hearts all the words He had spoken, that they might remember them.

JESUS AND
THE MULTITUDE

Now Jesus took His disciples and went aside privately into a desert place belonging to the city called Bethsaida.

And the people, when they knew it, followed Him; and He received them and spoke unto them of the kingdom of God, and healed them that had need of healing.

And when the day began to wear away, then came the Twelve, and they said unto Him, "Send the multitude away, that they may go into the towns and country round about, and lodge and get victuals; for we are here in a desert place."

But He said unto them, "Give them to eat."

And they said, "We have no more than five loaves and two fishes." For there were about five thousand people.

And He said unto His disciples, "Make them sit down by fifties, in a company."

And they did so and made them all sit down. Then he took the five loaves and the two fishes; and looking up to Heaven, He blessed them, and broke, and gave to the disciples to set before the multitude.

And they did eat and were filled; and there was taken up fragments that were left to the amount of twelve baskets.

And the people marveled exceedingly.

Now it came to pass that Jesus 'went into the temple in Jerusalem early in the morning, and the multitude came unto Him and He taught them. Then also came the learned men of the city, the scribes. They brought unto Him a woman who had sinned, and they said unto Jesus:

"Moses in the law commanded us that such as this woman should be stoned, even unto death; but what do You say?"

This they said, tempting Him, that they might accuse Him of breaking the ancient law and so harm Him. But Jesus stooped down and with His finger wrote on the ground, as though He heard them not.

And when they continued asking Him, He lifted Himself up, and said unto them, "He among you who has done no wrong, he that is without sin among you, let him cast the first stone."

And when they heard it, each knew that in his heart was some of evil, even as in the heart of the woman. And they went out one by one, and they did her no hurt. And the woman was left standing before Jesus.

When Jesus lifted Himself up and saw none but the woman, He said unto her, "Woman, where are those that would stone you, even unto death? Has none accused you?"

And she said, "No man, Lord."

And Jesus said, "Neither do I accuse you. Go, and sin no more."

And Jesus went and sat by the Sea of Galilee. And many were gathered unto Him, and He went into a ship and sat; and the whole multitude stood on the shore.

And He spoke, saying:

"Behold, a sower went forth to sow. And when he sowed, some seeds fell by the wayside, and fowls came and devoured them. Some fell upon stony places, where they had not much earth; and forthwith they sprung up. And when the sun was up, they were scorched. Because they had no roots, they withered away. And some fell among thorns; and the thorns sprang up and choked them. But others fell into good ground and brought forth fruit, some a hundredfold, some sixtyfold, some thirtyfold. Who has ears, let him hear."

Then did Jesus declare the meaning of the parable.

And He spoke unto them, how those that hear yet understand not, and those that see yet are blind before the truth, are like the seed that withered away.

"But the seed that fell into good ground is the man that hears the word and understands it; which also bears fruit and brings forth good deeds, some a hundredfold, some sixty, some thirty."

THE SERMON
ON THE MOUNT

And Jesus went up into a mountain; and His disciples came to Him, and a great multitude. And He taught them, saying:

Blessed are the poor in spirit:
For theirs is the kingdom of heaven.
Blessed are they that mourn:
For they shall be comforted.
Blessed are the gentle:
For they shall inherit the earth.
Blessed are they who hunger and thirst
after righteousness;
For they shall be filled.

Blessed are the merciful:
For they shall obtain mercy.
Blessed are the pure in heart:
For they shall see God.
Blessed are the peace-makers:
For they shall be called the children of God.
Blessed are they that are persecuted
    for righteousness:
For theirs is the kingdom of heaven.

And Jesus said, "Your Father knows what things you have need of before you ask Him. After this manner, therefore, pray you:

Our Father which art in heaven,
Hallowed be Thy name
Thy kingdom come.
Thy will be done
In earth as it is in Heaven.
Give us this day our daily bread.
And forgive us our debts,
As we forgive our debtors.
And lead us not into temptation,
But deliver us from evil;
For Thine is the kingdom,
And the power, and the glory,
For ever. Amen.

"For if you forgive men their wrongs against you, your Heavenly Father will also forgive you; but if you forgive men not, neither will your Father forgive you.

"Not everyone that says unto Me, 'Lord, Lord,' shall enter into the kingdom of Heaven; but he that does the will of My Father in Heaven. Therefore, whosoever hears these sayings of Mine and makes of them good works, I will liken him unto a wise man, who built his house upon a rock. The rain descended and the floods came, and the winds blew and beat upon that house; and it fell not. And everyone that hears these sayings of Mine and makes of them no good works, shall be likened unto a foolish man which built his house upon the sand, and the rain descended and the floods came, and the winds blew and beat upon that house; and it fell; and great was the fall of it."

113

And it came to pass, that the people brought Jesus young children, that He would touch them. But His disciples rebuked the people and sent them away.

And when Jesus saw it, He was much displeased and said unto them, "Suffer the little children to come unto Me, and forbid them not; for of such is the kingdom of heaven.

"Verily I say unto you, Whosoever shall not receive the kingdom of God as a little child, shall not enter therein."

And He took the children in His arms, and put His hands upon them, and blessed them.

THE PARABLE OF
THE PRODIGAL SON

Now fear was in the hearts of the elders and the governors of the land because of the multitudes that followed Jesus. And the governors wondred and questioned, saying, "Does this man come as King of the Jews; and shall we then be put down from our high places because of Him and because of those that follow in His way?"

And they plotted against His life and thought how they could harm the Son of Man, as Jesus called Himself. Jesus knew in what peril He walked, but He went about His Father's business, and continued to teach, saying:

"A certain man had two sons; and the younger of them said to his father, 'Father, give me the portion of goods that falls to me.' And the man divided his living between his two sons. And not many days after, the younger son gathered all together, and took his journey into a far country. There he wasted all that he had, for no good thing. And when he had spent all that he had, there arose a mighty famine in that land, and he began to be in want. And he went and joined himself to a man of that country; and the man sent him into his fields to tend swine.

"And the younger son wished that like the swine he might eat husks from the grain; for no man gave food unto him.

"And when he came to himself, he said, 'How many hired servants of my father's have bread enough and to spare, and I perish with hunger! I will arise and go to my father, and will say unto him, "Father, I have sinned against Heaven and before you, and am no more worthy to be called your son. Make me as one of your hired servants.'"

"And he arose and came to his father. But when he was yet a great way off, his father saw him, and had pity, and ran and fell on his neck and kissed him. And the son said unto him, 'Father, I have sinned against Heaven and in your sight, and am no more worthy to be called your son.' But the father said to his servants, 'Bring forth the best robe and put it on him; and put a ring on his hand and shoes on his feet; and bring hither the fatted calf and kill it; and let us eat and be merry. For this, my son, was dead and is alive again; he was lost and is found.' And they began to make merry.

"Now the elder son was in the field, and as he came and drew near to the house, he heard music and dancing. And he was angry, and said to his father, 'Lo, these many years have I served you, never going against your commandments; and yet you never gave me a lamb that I might make merry with my friends; but as soon as this son was come that wasted all that he had, you killed the fatted calf.'

"And his father said unto him, 'Son, you were ever with me, and all that I have is yours. It was right that we should make merry and be glad, for this your brother was dead, and is alive again; and was lost and is found.'"

JESUS ENTERS JERUSALEM

And it came to pass that Jesus and His disciples were going up to Jerusalem. And He spoke to the Twelve, His Apostles, and began to tell them what things should happen to Him, saying: "Behold, we go up to Jerusalem, and the Son of Man shall be delivered unto the chief priests, and unto the governors; and they shall bring about His death."

And when they came near Jerusalem at the Mount of Olives, Jesus sent forth two of His disciples, and said unto them:

"Go your way into the village which is near; and as soon as you have entered into it, you shall find a colt tied; loose him and bring him."

And they did as Jesus commanded them. They cast their garments on the colt, and Jesus sat upon them. And many spread garments in the way, and cut down branches and strewed them, crying, "Hosanna! Blessed is He that cometh in the name of the Lord! Hosanna in the highest!"

Now after two days was the Feast of the Passover; and the chief priests and the governors thought how they might take Jesus and put Him to death. And one of the Twelve Apostles, called Judas Iscariot, went unto the chief priests and said, "What will you give me, if I betray Jesus to you?" And they promised him thirty pieces of silver. And Judas said, "Whomever I shall kiss is He; hold Him fast."

On the first day of the unleavened bread, the disciples made ready the Passover. When evening came, Jesus took bread, and blessed, and broke it, and gave it to the disciples, and said: "Take, eat; this is My body." And He took the cup, and gave thanks, and gave it to them and said, "Drink ye all of it; for this is My blood of the New Testament, which is shed for many for the forgiveness of sins."

THE CRUCIFIXION

Now Jesus had gone into a place called Geth-semane to pray. And having prayed, He said to Peter and James and John, who were watching with Him, "Rise, let us be going. He who will betray Me is at hand."

And while He was speaking, Judas came with the soldiers of the city priests and elders. And he went to Jesus and kissed Him. And Jesus said unto him, "Friend, why are you here?"

Then the soldiers set hands on Jesus and took Him to the Roman ruler, Pontius Pilate, that Pilate might be His judge. Pilate questioned Him and said, "I can find no evil in this man."

But the crowd shouted, "Crucify Him! Cru-cify Him!" And Pilate washed his hands before the multitude, saying, "I am innocent of the blood of this just person." Yet he said that what they asked for would be done.

They scourged Him and mocked Him and crowned Him with thorns. And when they had brought Him unto a place called Golgotha, they nailed Him to a cross and crucified Him.

And Jesus said, "Father, forgive them; for they know not what they do."

After this, Jesus knew all things were come to pass, and now was the prophecy fulfilled; and He said, "It is finished."

And when the ninth hour had come, He cried with a loud voice, saying, "Father, into Thy hands I commend My spirit."

And, behold, the earth did quake, and the rocks broke. And when they that were watching Jesus saw the earthquake, they feared greatly, and they spoke, saying, "Truly, this was the Son of God!"

THE RESURRECTION

Now when it was evening there came a rich man of Arimathea named Joseph. He went to Pilate and asked for the body of Jesus. And when Joseph had taken the body, he wrapped it in a clean linen cloth, and laid it in his own new tomb which he had carved out from the rock, and he rolled a great stone to the door of the tomb, and departed.

After the Sabbath, toward the dawn of the first day of the week, Mary Magdalene, and Mary, the mother of Jesus, came to the tomb. And behold, the angel of the Lord descended from Heaven and came and rolled back the stone from the door and sat upon it. His countenance was like lightning, and his robe was white as snow; and those that watched were struck dumb with terror.

And the angel spoke, and said unto the women: "Fear not; for I know that you seek Jesus Who was crucified. He is not here; for He is risen, as He said. Come, see the place where the Lord lay. And go quickly and tell His disciples that He is risen from the dead. And behold, He goes before you into Galilee; there shall you see Him. Lo, I have told you."

And they departed from the tomb with fear and joy, and ran to bring the disciples word.

Then the Apostles went away unto Galilee into a mountain where Jesus had bidden them come. And they saw Jesus, and worshiped Him.

And it came to pass, while He blessed them, that He was parted from them, and carried up into heaven.

And they worshiped Him, and returned to Jerusalem with joy. For they had seen their Lord risen from the dead. And they remembered the words which Jesus spoke unto them, saying:

"Thus it is written in the law of Moses and in the prophets and in the psalms concerning Me. Peace be unto you! All power is given unto Me in Heaven and earth. Lo, I am with you always, even unto the end of the world. Amen."

CONTENTS

PREFACE

This volume is one of twenty Units produced by ILPAC, the Independent Learning Project for Advanced Chemistry, written for students preparing for the Advanced Level examinations of the G.C.E. The Project has been sponsored by the Inner London Education Authority and the materials have been extensively tested in London schools and colleges. In its present revised form, however, it is intended for a wider audience; the syllabuses of all the major Examination Boards have been taken into account and questions set by these boards have been included.

Although ILPAC was initially conceived as a way of overcoming some of the difficulties presented by uneconomically small sixth forms, it has frequently been adopted because its approach to learning has certain advantages over more traditional teaching methods. Students assume a greater responsibility for their own learning and can work, to some extent, at their own pace, while teachers can devote more time to guiding individual students and to managing resources.

By providing personal guidance, and detailed solutions to the many exercises, supported by the optional use of video-cassettes, the Project allows students to study A-level chemistry with less teacher-contact time than a conventional course demands. The extent to which this is possible must be determined locally; potentially hazardous practical work must, of course, be supervised. Nevertheless, flexibility in time-tabling makes ILPAC an attractive proposition in situations where classes are small or suitably-qualified teachers are scarce.

In addition, ILPAC can provide at least a partial solution to other problems. Students with only limited access to laboratories, for example, those studying at evening classes, can concentrate upon ILPAC practical work in the laboratory, in the confidence that related theory can be systematically studied elsewhere. Teachers of A-level chemistry who are inexperienced, or whose main discipline is another science, will find ILPAC very supportive. The materials can be used effectively where upper and lower sixth form classes are timetabled together. ILPAC can provide 'remedial' material for students in higher education. Schools operating sixth form consortia can benefit from the cohesion that ILPAC can provide in a fragmented situation. The project can be adapted for use in parts of the world where there is a severe shortage of qualified chemistry teachers. And so on.

A more detailed introduction to ILPAC, with specific advice both to students and to teachers, is included in the first volume only. Details of the Project Team and Trial Schools appear inside the back cover.

LONDON 1983

ACKNOWLEDGEMENTS

Thanks are due to the following examination boards for permission to
reproduce questions from past A-level papers:

Joint Matriculation Board:
   Teacher-marked Exercise p191(1978)

Oxford Delegacy of Local Examinations;
   Exercise 32(1977)
   Teacher-marked Exercises p121(1980), p20-part2(1981), part3(1980)
   End-of-Unit Test 21(1979)

Southern Universities Joint Board;
   Exercise 21(1978)

The Associated Examining Board;
   End-of-Unit Test 23(1981)

University of London Entrance and School Examinations Council
   Exercises 2(N1981), 10(L1981), 43(N1974), 44(N1976)
   Teacher-marked Exercises p20-part1(N1982), p23(N1976), p32(N1980),
                       p63(L1977)
   End-of-Unit Test 1-6(L1981), 7-10(N1978), 11(N1977), 12(N1980),
                13 & 14(N1979), 15(L1975), 16(N1979), 17(N1980),
                18(L1982), 19(N1981), 20(N1979), 22(L1982)

Welsh Joint Education Committee
   Exercises 22(1979), 30(1977 & 1979), 41(1979)
   End-of-Unit Test 24(1976), 25(1979)

Questions from papers of other examining boards appear in other Units.

Where answers to these questions are included, they are provided by ILPAC
and not by the examination boards.

Photographs are included by permission as follows:

Cover centre, DNA model - Professor M.H.F. Wilkins, Biophysics Dept., King's
                       College, London.
Fig. 2, nylon fibre production, and Fig. 4, polyester sails -
   Keystone Press Agency Ltd.
Fig. 5, rubber-tapping - Popperfoto Ltd.
Fig. 7, PVC shoe production, Fig. 8, expanded polystyrene packaging, and
   Fig. 9, kitchen plastics - Shell photographs.
Fig. 11, sickle-cells - Biophoto Associates.
Photographs of students and those on pages 21 and 37 - Tony Langham

Fig. 15 is based on a drawing in 'Advancing Chemistry' by M. Lewis &
   G. Waller, Oxford University Press.
Fig. 17 is reproduced by courtesy of Professor D.C. Phillips, FRS
Fig. 18 is reproduced from 'Biological Chemistry' by H.R. Mahler and
   E.H. Cordes, Harper & Row, New York, (after C.C.F. Blake, D.F. Koenig,
   G.A. Mair, A.C.T. North, D.C. Phillips, V.C. Sarma - Nature, 206:757(1965).
Fig. 27 is from Cell Structure and Function, 2nd edition, by Ariel G. Loewy
   and Philip Siekevitz. Copyright (c) 1963, 1969 by Holt, Rinehart and
   Winston, Inc. Reprinted by permission of Holt, Rinehart and Winston,
   CBS College Publishing.
Fig. 36 is reproduced by courtesy of Dr. J.P.G. Richards, University College,
   Cardiff.

SYMBOLS USED IN ILPAC UNITS

 Reading

 Exercise

 Test

 'A' Level question

 'A' Level part question

 'A' Level question Special paper

 Worked example

 Teacher-marked exercise

 Revealing exercises

 Discussion

 Computer programme

 Experiment

 Video programme

 Film loop

 Model-making

INTERNATIONAL HAZARD SYMBOLS

 Harmful

 Flammable

 Corrosive

 Toxic

 Explosive

 Oxidising

 Radioactive

INTRODUCTION

This Unit is about big molecules of various types and sizes, excluding the giant ionic and molecular lattices which you have already studied in Unit S4 (Structure and Bonding).

In Level One we consider first some of the ways in which big molecules known as synthetic polymers can be built up from simple molecules known as monomers. We distinguish different kinds of synthetic polymer by their properties and by the types of reaction employed in their production.

At the end of Level One we discuss the structures, properties and relative merits of soapy and soapless detergents.

In Level Two we look at some naturally-occurring big molecules, particularly proteins and polysaccharides, but we also discuss the monomers or sub-units from which they are made, namely amino acids and sugars. At the end of Level Two we discuss very briefly nucleic acids (DNA and RNA) and lipids, which are also very important in biological systems.

In an Appendix, we provide a simple treatment of X-ray crystallography.

Syllabus requirements vary very widely in this area of chemistry. Before you start this Unit, find out from your teacher which sections you need to study.

There are four experiments in Level Two of this Unit and one more advanced experiment in an Appendix.

There are two video-programmes designed to accompany this Unit. They are not essential but you should try to see them at the appropriate times if they are available.

Instrumental Techniques

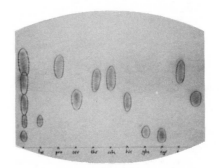

Organic Techniques 3

Overleaf is a table which shows you the range of molecular mass of the substances we mention in this Unit.

A table of size comparisons

Type of structure	Example(s)	Relative molecular mass
Simple molecule	Carbon dioxide, CO_2	44
	Octadec-9-enoic acid (oleic acid), $C_{17}H_{33}CO_2H$	266
Large molecule	Tristearin (a fat), $C_{57}H_{110}O_6$	890
Protein	Insulin	5 733
	Human haemoglobin	64 500
	Urease	473 000
	Snail haemoglobin	6 700 000
	Tobacco mosaic virus	40 000 000
Polysaccharide	Amylose	20 000 to 500 000
	Amylopectin	up to 1 000 000
Synthetic polymer	Polyethene (low density)	50 000 to 300 000
	(high density)	up to 3 000 000
Nucleic acid	DNA	up to 10 000 000 000

PRE-KNOWLEDGE

Before you start on this Unit you should have studied Units 01, 02 and 03 and also should be able to:

(1)   explain the term 'hard water';

(2)   describe the effect of hard water on soap;

(3)   write structural formulae for two complex ions of copper;

(4)   describe the action of a buffer solution;

(5)   derive and use the expression:

$$pH = pK_a - \log \frac{[acid]}{[base]}$$

PRE-TEST

To find out whether you are ready to start Level One, try the following test, which is based on the pre-knowledge items. You should not spend more than 20 minutes on this test. Hand your answers to your teacher for marking.

Big Molecules

© Inner London Education Authority 1984

First published 1984
by John Murray (Publishers) Ltd
50 Albemarle Street, London W1X 4BD

Printed in Great Britain by
Martin's of Berwick

British Library Cataloguing in Publication Data

Independent Learning Project for Advanced Chemistry
  Big molecules. - (ILPAC; unit 04)
  1. Science
  I. Title   II. Series
  500   Q161.2

ISBN 0 7195 4048 8

PRE-TEST

1. (a) Name two substances which make water 'hard'. (2)

   (b) Using the formula NaSp to represent a soap, write an
       equation for the reaction between soap and hard water. (2)

2. Write structural formulae for the following complex ions and
   state their shapes:

   (a) tetraamminecopper(II), (2)

   (b) tetrachlorocuprate(II). (2)

3. (a) Write a simple definition of a buffer solution in terms
       of its function. (2)

   (b) Name two types of substance (in addition to water!) found
       in most buffer solutions. (2)

4. Use the equilibrium law to derive the expression for the pH of a
   buffer solution:

   $$pH = pK_a - \log \frac{[acid]}{[base]}$$ (4)

   (Total 16 marks)

LEVEL ONE

POLYMERS

Big molecules of the simplest type are known as polymers, because they consist of many identical units bonded together. Synthetic polymers are made by reactions between individual units (monomers) and we can classify them as addition or condensation polymers according to the type of reaction.

You have met some examples in earlier Units (polyethene, Terylene, Bakelite, nylon); now you apply your knowledge of addition and condensation reactions to some further examples of each type, beginning with addition polymers.

Addition polymers

Objectives. When you have finished this section you should be able to:

(1) show how addition polymers are related to ethene, and write equations for the formation of some examples;

(2) describe a mechanism for the formation of an addition polymer;

(3) distinguish between atactic and isotactic polymers.

The most common type of addition polymer is based on ethene. One (or more) of the hydrogen atoms may be substituted by another group so that the generalised equation for the formation of an addition polymer is:

$$n \quad \overset{H}{\underset{H}{}}\!\!C=C\!\!\overset{H}{\underset{Y}{}} \quad \rightarrow \quad \left(\begin{array}{cc} H & H \\ | & | \\ C & C \\ | & | \\ H & Y \end{array} \right)_n$$

Find a textbook which covers addition polymers and skim the whole section. Look for a range of polymers that are substituted ethenes and the free radical mechanism for their formation. In particular, notice which substances act as catalysts in the reactions. It would also be useful to look back through your earlier notes on addition polymers that you made on Unit 01 (Hydrocarbons).

In the exercise which follows, you examine a range of addition polymers which are all substituted ethenes.

Exercise 1   Complete a copy of Table 1, which lists the side-chain
              groups found in the most common ethene-based polymers.
              Note that the trimers are included only to help you
              understand the structures - normally n = several hundreds
              or even thousands.

Table 1 Ethene-based polymers

Group Y in monomer $CH_2=CHY$	Structural formula of trimer (n = 3)	Repeating unit	Name(s)
$-H$	$H-\overset{H}{\underset{H}{C}}-\overset{H}{\underset{H}{C}}-\overset{H}{\underset{H}{C}}-\overset{H}{\underset{H}{C}}-\overset{H}{\underset{H}{C}}-\overset{H}{\underset{H}{C}}-H$	$-\overset{H}{\underset{H}{C}}-\overset{H}{\underset{H}{C}}-$	
$-CH_3$			
$-Cl$			
$-CN$			
⬡			
$-O-\overset{\overset{O}{\|\|}}{C}\diagdown_{CH_3}$			

(Answers on page 84)

In the next exercise you carry out the reverse process - deciding which
monomer gives rise to a particular polymer.

Exercise 2   Which of the monomers A to D could give rise to the
              addition polymer shown below?

$$-\overset{H}{\underset{CH_3}{C}}-\overset{H}{\underset{H}{C}}-\overset{CH_3}{\underset{H}{C}}-\overset{H}{\underset{H}{C}}-\overset{H}{\underset{CH_3}{C}}-\overset{H}{\underset{H}{C}}-\overset{H}{\underset{CH_3}{C}}-\overset{H}{\underset{H}{C}}-$$

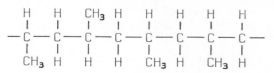

A $\overset{H}{\underset{H}{}}C=C\overset{CH_3}{\underset{H}{}}$

B $H_3C\diagdown C=\overset{H}{\underset{}{C}}-\overset{H}{\underset{H}{C}}-CH_3$

C $\overset{H}{\underset{H}{}}C=\overset{}{C}-\overset{H}{\underset{CH_3}{C}}=C\overset{H}{\underset{H}{}}$

D $\overset{H}{\underset{H_3C}{}}C=C\overset{CH_3}{\underset{H}{}}$

E $\overset{H}{\underset{H}{}}C=\overset{}{C}-\overset{CH_3}{\underset{CH_3}{C}}=C\overset{H}{\underset{H}{}}$

(Answer on page 84)

As you know from Unit 01, many addition reactions take place by a
free radical mechanism. We explore such a reaction in the following
revealing exercise.

Q1. Di(benzenecarbonyl) peroxide (benzoyl peroxide) has the formula:

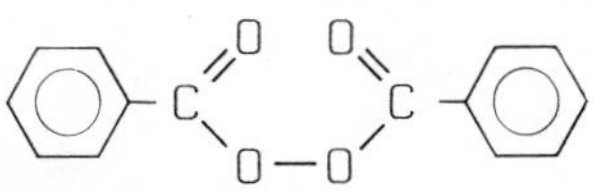

It is commonly used as an initiator in chain reactions. The molecule can be split homolytically into two identical radicals. Write down the formula of the radical.

A1.

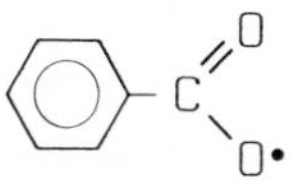

(leading to  • + CO_2)

Q2. Using R• to stand for the radical, write an equation for the initiation step in the polymerization of phenylethene (styrene). Assume that R• attacks the CH_2 group rather than the CH group.

A2. 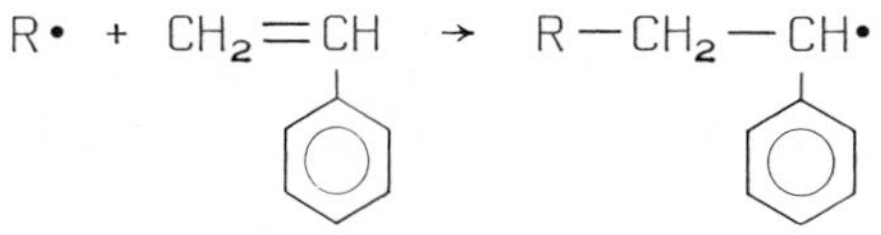 R• + CH_2=CH → R—CH_2—CH•

Q3. Write an equation to show how the product shown in A2 could react with another molecule of styrene.

A3. 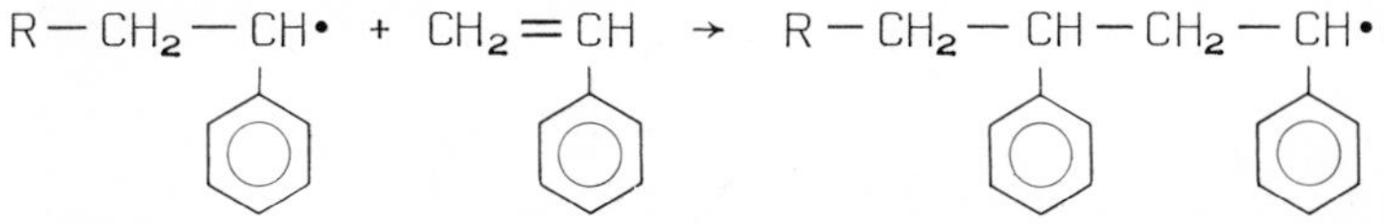 R—CH_2—CH• + CH_2=CH → R—CH_2—CH—CH_2—CH•

Q4. After any number of such propagation steps, the chain may be terminated in several different ways. State in words (no formulae) the types of particle which could react together in three possible termination steps.

A4. (a) Two initiating radicals.

(b) An initiating radical and a partly-polymerized chain.

(c) Two partly-polymerized chains.

Q5. Write an equation to show reaction (b).

A5. 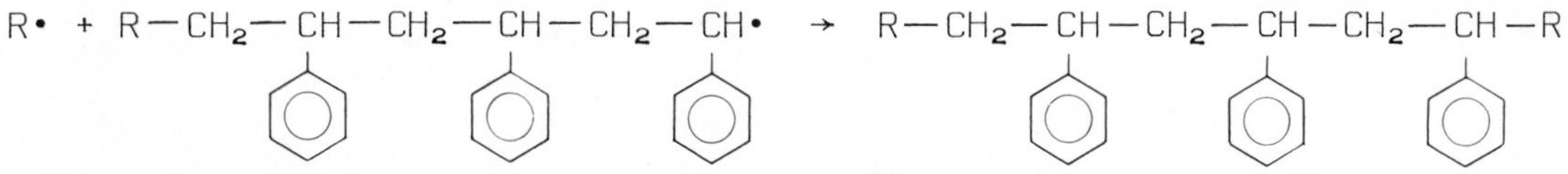 R• + R—CH_2—CH—CH_2—CH—CH_2—CH• → R—CH_2—CH—CH_2—CH—CH_2—CH—R

Q6. Why is the term 'catalyst' not strictly applicable to the initiator?

A6. Catalysts are regenerated in the course of a reaction.

Note that the presence of R groups at the ends of each chain means that the formula of the polymer is not completely represented by the formula $(-CH_2-CHC_6H_5-)_n$. However, the discrepancy is not important because n is so large.

7

The Ziegler-Natta catalysts (aluminium alkyls with a titanium compound), which you met in Unit 01 when you studied the polymerization of ethene and propene, operate by an ionic mechanism. However, we suggest that you need not concern yourself with the details.

Now we look at some different ways in which the monomer units may be arranged along a polymer chain.

Isotactic and atactic polymers

In most polymers the monomer units always link together 'head-to-tail', as shown in the Revealing Exercise. However, this type of addition does not necessarily give such an ordered structure as you might think at first by looking at 'flat' formulae with straight chains like those we have used so far.

Bonds occur in tetrahedral directions around each carbon atom, and alternate carbon atoms are asymmetric (attached to four different atoms or groups). This means that two different orientations are possible for each monomer unit added. Consequently, there is a large number of stereoisomers but, fortunately, you need consider two types only.

Read about the structural difference between isotactic and atactic polymers so that you can do the next exercise.

Exercise 3 (a) Structures A and B represent portions of polymer chains. Classify each as atactic or isotactic.

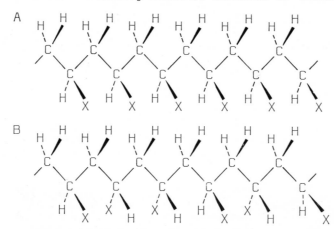

(b) Free radical mechanisms generally give atactic polymers while ionic mechanisms generally give isotactic polymers. From your knowledge of the reaction conditions during manufacture, would you expect polyphenylethene and poly-propene to be isotactic or atactic?

(Answers on page 84)

As you might expect, isotactic and atactic versions of the same polymer show differences in some physical properties. We return to this point later. First we consider some polymers formed by condensation reactions between monomer molecules.

x

8

Condensation polymers - polyamides and polyesters

Objectives. When you have finished this section you should be able to:

(4) quote some examples of condensation polymers and write equations to show their formation;

(5) state the difference between a homopolymer and a copolymer.

Start by reading about condensation polymers in a textbook, looking out for the difference between copolymers and homopolymers, and for the types of reaction by which they are formed. You may also wish to revise work from Units 02 and 03 where you studied the condensation reactions between —OH and —CO$_2$H and between —NH$_2$ and —CO$_2$H.

You should now be able to do the next exercise which is the first of several on polyamides.

Exercise 4   Fig. 1 shows a molecule containing both an amino group and a carboxylic acid group. The box represents a carbon skeleton separating the two groups.

$$H_2N-\boxed{}-CO_2H$$

Fig. 1.

(a) Write an equation to show how three such molecules might join together in a condensation reaction. (Don't worry about reaction conditions at this stage.)

(b) What name is given to the structural unit linking the boxes?

(Answers on page 84)

The reaction you have just outlined is the basis of one form of nylon, nylon-11. This uses the 11 carbon molecule NH$_2$(CH$_2$)$_{10}$CO$_2$H, 11-amino undecanoic acid (the name nylon-11 refers to the 11 carbon atoms). In the next exercise you examine a reaction which gives another form of nylon.

Fig. 2. Nylon fibres during manufacture

Exercise 5   Fig. 3 shows two molecules which together can form a
condensation polymer.

$$H_2N \boxed{} NH_2 \qquad\qquad HO_2C \boxed{} CO_2H$$

Fig. 3.

(a)   Write an equation to show how two such molecules might
join together.

(b)   If the reaction continued, a polymer chain would be produced.
Write down the formula of the repeating unit.

(c)   Explain the meaning of the terms 'copolymer' and 'homopolymer', using the polymer you have just written about and
the one in the previous exercise as illustrations.

(Answers on page 84)

When each of the molecules in the previous exercise contain six carbon atoms,
polymerization leads to nylon-66:

$$n\,NH_2(CH_2)_6NH_2 + n\,CO_2H(CH_2)_4CO_2H \rightarrow \left(-\!\!\begin{array}{c}H\\|\\N\end{array}\!\!-(CH_2)_6-\!\!\begin{array}{c}H\\|\\N\end{array}\!\!-\!\!\begin{array}{c}\\C\\||\\O\end{array}\!\!-(CH_2)_4-\!\!\begin{array}{c}O\\||\\C\end{array}\!\!-\right)_n + 2n\,H_2O$$

repeating unit of nylon-66

A third method of producing nylon involves a substance called caprolactam.
This can be regarded as an internal amide of 6-aminohexanoic acid:

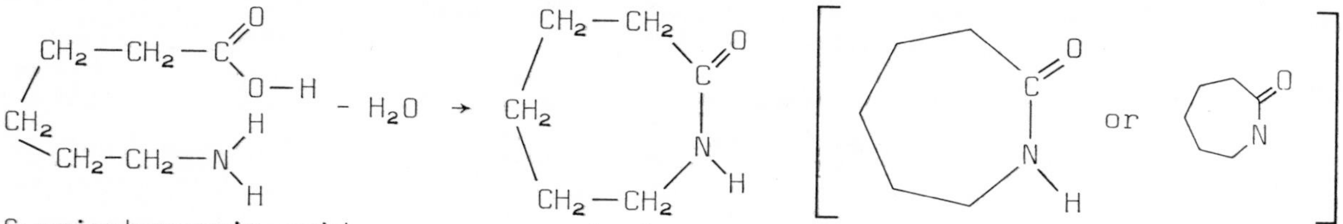

6-aminohexanoic acid   caprolactam   or

Like 1,6-diaminohexane and 1,6-hexanedioic acid, caprolactam is made
commercially from cyclohexane.

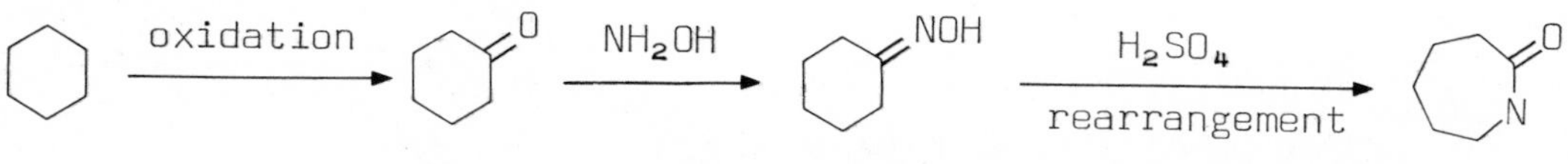

oxidation → ... NH₂OH → ... H₂SO₄ rearrangement → ...

During polymerization the rings re-open and then link together in long
chains.

Exercise 6   (a)   Write the formula of the repeating unit in the homopolymer made from caprolactam.

(b)   What is the name given to this type of nylon?

(Answers on page 84)

Now test your understanding of polyamide formation by attempting the
following exercises.

10

Exercise 7   Choose, from the following list of monomers, those which
              could polymerize to give each of the structures A, B an C.
              Which are copolymers and which are homopolymers?

1. $NH_2CH_2CH_2NH_2$ 4. $NH_2CH_2CHCO_2H$
                                         $|$
2. $NH_2CH_2CH_2CO_2H$ CH_3

3. $CO_2HCH_2CH_2CO_2H$ 5. $NH_2CH_2CHCH_2CO_2H$
                                         $|$
                                         CH_3

A
$$NH_2-CH_2-CH_2-\overset{\overset{O}{\|}}{C}-\underset{\underset{H}{|}}{N}-CH_2-CH_2-\overset{\overset{O}{\|}}{C}-\underset{\underset{H}{|}}{N}-CH_2-CH_2-\overset{\overset{O}{\|}}{C}-\underset{\underset{H}{|}}{N}-CH_2-CH_2-\overset{\overset{O}{\|}}{C}-OH$$

B
$$NH_2-CH_2-CH_2-\underset{\underset{H}{|}}{N}-\overset{\overset{O}{\|}}{C}-CH_2-CH_2-\overset{\overset{O}{\|}}{C}-\underset{\underset{H}{|}}{N}-CH_2-CH_2-\underset{\underset{H}{|}}{N}-\overset{\overset{O}{\|}}{C}-CH_2-CH_2-\overset{\overset{O}{\|}}{C}-OH$$

C
$$NH_2-CH_2-\underset{\underset{CH_3}{|}}{CH}-\overset{\overset{O}{\|}}{C}-\underset{\underset{H}{|}}{N}-CH_2-\underset{\underset{CH_3}{|}}{CH}-\overset{\overset{O}{\|}}{C}-\underset{\underset{H}{|}}{N}-CH_2-\underset{\underset{CH_3}{|}}{CH}-\overset{\overset{O}{\|}}{C}-\underset{\underset{H}{|}}{N}-CH_2-\underset{\underset{CH_3}{|}}{CH}-\overset{\overset{O}{\|}}{C}-OH$$

(Answers on page 84)

Exercise 8   Which one of the following pairs of compounds might
              be made to combine together, under suitable conditions,
              to form a polyamide?

A   ammonia and a monocarboxylic acid

B   a mono-amine and a monocarboxylic acid

C   a diamine and a monocarboxylic acid

D   a mono-amine and a dicarboxylic acid

E   a dicarboxylic acid and a diamine

(Answer on page 84)

We now consider another type
of condensation polymer –
polyesters. Start by
reading the section on
polyesters in your textbook
to help you do the following
exercises.

Fig. 4. Most sails are now made of polyester

11

Exercise 9 (a) Write an equation to show how a trimer could be formed from the following three molecules:

HO_2C —⟨○⟩— CO_2H $2CH_2OH$ CH_2OH

benzene 1,4-dicarboxylic   ethane-1,2-diol
acid (terephthalic acid)   (ethylene glycol)

(b) What type of linkage is formed between the molecules?

(c) Which well-known polyester is formed by a similar reaction?

(Answers on page 84)

Exercise 10 Which of the following would react together, in pairs, to form a polymer?

1. $HOCH_2CH_2OH$ and $HO_2CCH_2CH_2CO_2H$

2. $HO_2CCH_2CH_2CO_2H$ and $HO(CH_2)_4CO_2H$

3. $HO(CH_2)_6OH$ and $ClOC(CH_2)_4COCl$

4. $HO_2C(CH_2)_4OH$ and $HOCH_2CH_2OH$

(Answer on page 85)

To help consolidate your knowledge about the two main types of polymer, attempt the following Teacher-marked Exercise. Look through your notes and make a rough plan before you start writing.

Teacher-marked Exercise   Explain what you understand by the terms addition polymerization and condensation polymerization, illustrating each answer with an example.

All the polymers you have considered so far have one thing in common - each consists mainly of unbranched chains. We now take a look at polymers formed from monomers with three reactive sites per molecule. These can form multi-dimensional polymers with branched or cross-linked chains.

Bakelite - a cross-linked polymer

We have already mentioned Bakelite in Units 02 and 03 when discussing the uses of phenol and methanal, from which it is made. It was discovered in the 1870's (probably the first modern 'plastic') and has been widely used ever since 1907 when Baekeland took out the first patents in New York. Other polymers with superior properties have been developed but Bakelite is cheap and is used as an insulator of both heat and electricity in applications where its brittleness and dark colour are not serious drawbacks.

Objectives. When you have finished this section you should be able to:

(6) give an example of a cross-linked polymer;

(7) describe the effect of cross-linking on the physical properties of a polymer.

Start by reading about <u>Bakelite</u> looking, in particular, for an
explanation of its <u>insolubility</u> and brittle nature. You may find it
called <u>phenol-methanal polymer</u>, or <u>PF (phenol-formaldehyde) resin</u>.

In the first stage of the reaction between phenol and methanal, phenol is
substituted at the 2,4 and 6 positions of the ring. In the next exercise
you suggest which products are formed.

<u>Exercise 11</u> (a) Write an equation to show how one molecule of
methanal could react with one molecule of phenol.

(b) Do you think this reaction proceeds by nucleophilic
or electrophilic attack? Explain.

(c) Write the formulae of products that would be formed in
further reactions if there were plenty of methanal present
in the reaction mixture.

(Answers on page 85)

The reaction you have just described results in mono-, di- and tri-
substituted phenol molecules, depending on the relative amounts of phenol and
methanal present. In the next stage of the reaction, the phenol-alcohols
condense together (or with more phenol) to form chains, as described in the
following exercise.

<u>Exercise 12</u> Complete the equation below to show the formation of
a phenol-methanal trimer.

(Answer on page 85)

The last stage in the process is extensive cross-linking between long chains.
Under appropriate conditions this continues until each reactive site on each
phenol molecule is joined via a methylene ($-CH_2-$) group to another phenol
molecule. A possible arrangement is shown below but, in practice, the
structure would be three-dimensional and less regular than this.

13

Exercise 13   Why do you think Bakelite is hard, brittle and
              insoluble in all known solvents?

              (Answer on page 85)

You have probably heard of some other cross-linked polymers made from methanal
by condensation reactions. If carbamide (urea), NH_2CONH_2, is used in place
of phenol, carbamide-methanal resins can be made.

→ cross-linked resin containing
   $-N-CH_2-N-$ links.

These polymers are commonly known as urea-formaldehyde (UF) resins and they
have been used extensively in foam form for heat insulation, e.g. in cavity
walls. However, there have been serious health hazards in some faulty
installations because the foam can give off toxic methanal vapour. If you
are interested in reading about this, ask your teacher for some references.

Another well-known polymer is made from methanal and 2,4,6-triamino-
1,3,5-triazone, commonly called Melamine.

Each molecule has six possible sites for
condensation so that very extensive
cross-linking occurs. The product is
strong and heat-resistant, which makes it
suitable for tableware and tough laminates
such as Formica.

Extensive cross-linking in three dimensions results in rigid structures like
those mentioned above. A smaller degree of cross-linking is found in polymers known as rubbers, which we consider in the next section.

Rubber

Pure natural rubber is a long-chain
polymer made from the milky latex fluid
collected from rubber trees. It is of
little practical use because it is not
hard-wearing and becomes soft and sticky
when warm. It becomes much more useful
when the polymer chains are cross-
linked by a process called vulcanization.

Fig. 5. Tapping a rubber tree to obtain latex

14

Objectives. When you have finished this section you should be able to:

(8) describe how <u>rubber</u> is vulcanized;

(9) explain the effect of <u>vulcanization</u> on the properties of rubber.

Start by reading about natural rubber and the process called
vulcanization. Look for a description of how vulcanization changes
the properties of rubber.   Then do the next exercise.

<u>Exercise 14</u>   Natural rubber is a polymer of 2-methylbuta-1,3-diene.

A

(a) Write the structural formula of the monomer.

(b) Show the structure of a section of the polymer.

(c) How would you classify this polymer?

(d) In what way is the structure modified by vulcanization?

(e) What chemical substance is used to vulcanize rubber?

(f) What feature of the polymer chain enables vulcanization
to take place?

(g) How are the properties of natural rubber modified by
increasing degrees of vulcanization?

(Answers on page 85)

The uncertain supply of natural rubber, particularly in war-time, led to the
development of synthetic rubbers. Some of these have superior properties to
natural rubber, but are more expensive. They are related to natural rubber,
as indicated below.

$$CH_2=CH-C=CH_2$$
$$|$$
$$CH_3$$
2-methylbuta-1,3-diene   → natural rubber

$$CH_2=CH-C=CH_2$$
$$|$$
$$Cl$$
2-chlorobuta-1,3-diene   → Neoprene

$$CH_2=CH-CH=CH_2$$ → Buna rubber
buta-1,3-diene

$$CH_2=CH-CH=CH_2 + C_6H_5CH=CH_2$$ → Buna S rubber (SBR)
buta-1,3-diene   phenylethene   (a copolymer)

Ask your teacher whether you need to know more details of the
manufacture and special properties of these synthetic rubbers.
If so, you should be able to find what you want in a textbook.

You·have already seen some of the ways in which the physical properties of
polymers depend on their structure. In the next section we consider
physical properties in more detail.

Physical properties of polymers

In this section we take an overview of the properties of different polymers, including some of the more important terms used to describe them.

<u>Objectives</u>. When you have finished this section you should be able to:

(10) explain the meanings of the terms <u>thermosoftening</u> plastic (<u>thermoplastic</u>) and <u>thermosetting</u> plastic (<u>thermosett</u>), and quote some examples of each;

(11) list the structural factors which increase the <u>crystalline nature</u> of polymers;

(12) state the structural features found in a polymer which forms <u>fibres</u>;

(13) explain how fibres are formed and give examples of a fibre-forming polymer.

This area is well covered in the polymers section of many textbooks. Read the sections on physical properties and cross-linking. Now attempt the following exercises, parts of which are similar to A-level questions. The first one deals with thermoplastics and thermosetts.

<u>Exercise 15</u> (a) Phenylethene (styrene), $CH_2{=}CHC_6H_5$, polymerizes to form polyphenylethene (polystyrene) which is a thermoplastic. What is the meaning of the term 'thermoplastic'?

(b) How do the properties of a thermosetting plastic differ from those of a thermoplastic?

(c) Give an example of a thermosetting plastic.

(d) What are the important chemical changes which occur during thermosetting?

(Answers on page 85)

Most polymers, whether they are thermoplastic or thermosetting, do not appear to have any of the properties which you normally associate with crystals. However, polymer chains often do arrange themselves in a regularly-packed manner to give small crystallites separated by amorphous areas. This is shown diagrammatically in Fig. 6.

The more readily the individual chains can be aligned, the greater is the extent of crystalline character. You explore this idea in the next exercise.

Fig. 6.

Exercise 16 (a) What instrumental technique is used to detect the crystalline nature of certain polymers?

(b) Would you expect the following features to be associated with a high or a low degree of crystalline character in a polymer? Explain.

 (i) A regular 'head-to-tail' arrangement of monomer units.

 (ii) An atactic arrangement of the groups attached along the polymer chain.

 (iii) Large groups attached along the chain.

 (iv) A considerable amount of chain branching.

 (v) Extensive cross-linking between chains.

 (vi) Thermosetting properties.

(c) 'High density' polyethene is made using Ziegler-Natta catalysts which tend to produce long chains with hardly any branching. How does this affect its density and other properties?

(Answers on page 85)

Synthetic fibres have a high degree of crystallinity, but another factor also is important, as you show in the next exercise.

Exercise 17 Suggest reasons why polypropenenitrile (polyacrylo-nitrile) and nylon are suitable for use in textile fibres whereas polyphenylethene (polystyrene) and poly-ethene are not.

(Answer on page 86)

In the next section we consider the production of some important polymers.

Industrial production of polymers

At A-level, you may be required to know the outlines of selected manufacturing processes. (Precise details may be closely-guarded secrets belonging to the chemical company concerned.) Before you start this section, check with your teacher which processes you need to know for your particular syllabus.

Objectives. When you have finished this section you should be able to:

(14) outline the industrial production of some of the following:

 (a) polyphenylethene (polystyrene),
 (b) polyethene (polythene), low and high density forms,
 (c) polychloroethene (polyvinylchloride, PVC),
 (d) polytetrafluoroethene (PTFE),
 (e) nylon,
 (f) Terylene;

(15) state at least one use for each of the polymers listed above.

You should now read about, and make brief notes on, any processes mentioned in your syllabus. As a guide, look for the <u>conditions</u> needed: temperature, pressure and details of any catalyst used. Note how many stages there are in the process and whether there are any by-products, including any that are fed back into the main process. Another important aspect is the <u>uses</u> of the polymers - you need to know at least one main use for each polymer you study.

Also look for details of any <u>hazards</u> involved in the process, such as the use of carcinogenic (cancer-causing) substances. A case in point is the raw material for PVC manufacture, chloroethene (vinylchloride monomer), which was widely used for several years before its hazardous nature became apparent. Ask your teacher for some reading references.

Fig. 7. PVC shoes in an Indian factory

Fig. 8. Expanded polystyrene packaging

As you may have gathered from your reading, there are often several ways of making a particular product. Some of the factors that a chemical company might take into account in deciding which route to use for a particular product are:

   (a)   availability of raw materials,

   (b)   energy needed for the process,

   (c)   hazards to the workers,

   (d)   environmental pollution

The costs of raw materials, energy and labour vary from country to country and from time to time. Also variable are Government regulations, Trade Union strength and social attitudes to hazards and pollution. Consequently, different processes may be in use for the manufacture of the same product according to the conditions prevailing when the plant was planned.

The Teacher-marked Exercise which follows is about two alternative routes for PVC production. It is the sort of question where several different answers may be acceptable provided that the reasoning is sound. We suggest that you discuss the questions with other people in the group, and with your teacher. After you have sorted out your own ideas, write your answer to the question and hand it in to your teacher in the usual way.

Read the following account and answer the questions.

A

Chloroethene (vinyl chloride), used for the production of poly(chloroethene) (polyvinyl chloride) plastics, can be manufactured from ethyne by reaction with hydrogen chloride in the presence of mercury(II) chloride as catalyst.

$$CH \equiv CH + HCl \xrightarrow[200^{\circ}C]{HgCl_2} CH_2 = CHCl$$

The reaction is highly exothermic and temperature control is essential. Ethyne is obtained by the hydrolysis of calcium dicarbide; the latter is made by heating a mixture of coke and calcium oxide in an electric furnace at 2000 °C.

The ethyne process has now been large superseded by a route based on ethene. Thus, ethene and chlorine react to form 1,2-dichloroethane which is also used as a solvent for the following reaction.

$$CH_2 = CH_2 + Cl_2 \xrightarrow{50 \ ^{\circ}C} CH_2ClCH_2Cl$$

The product of this reaction is then decomposed by passing the vapour over a heated catalyst.

$$CH_2ClCH_2Cl \xrightarrow{500 \ ^{\circ}C} CH_2 = CHCl + HCl$$

The hydrogen chloride is re-used in an oxychlorination process yielding 1,2-dichloroethane.

$$CH_2 = CH_2 + \tfrac{1}{2}O_2 + 2HCl \rightarrow CH_2ClCH_2Cl + H_2O$$

Ethene is readily available from petroleum by cracking and chlorine is obtained by the electrolysis of brine.

It has recently been found that prolonged exposure to chloro-ethene can lead to cancer of the liver.

(a) For each process, identify as many advantageous and disadvantageous features as you can.

(b) Give a reason why the second route has superseded the first.

(c) Under what circumstances could the ethyne route become relatively more competitive?

(d) List some of the precautions which have to be taken during the production and use of chloroethene.

The next exercise concerns the production of polyphenylethene (polystyrene).

Exercise 18   The following reaction scheme shows a route for making phenylethene (styrene):

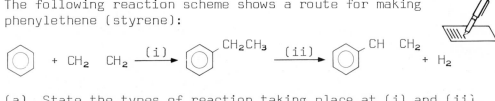

(a) State the types of reaction taking place at (i) and (ii).

(b) Give the conditions needed (catalyst and temperature) for each stage of the reaction.

(c) Finally, the styrene is polymerized by a free radical process. Name a suitable initiator for this reaction.

(Answers on page 86)

To sum up your work on polymers and help you consolidate your knowledge you should now attempt one of the questions in the following Teacher-marked Exercise. They are all examination questions; ask your teacher to help you decide which is most appropriate for you.

Teacher-marked   Choose <u>one</u> of the following three questions.
      Exercise

1. Write an essay on 'synthetic polymers'. Aspects which you might consider include:

   (a) the nature of the chemical reactions used to make the polymers,

   (b) the methods used for their fabrication,

   (c) some specific applications of polymers, and

   (d) the effect of structure on the properties of a polymer.

2. (a) Give one example of, and explain the constitution of (i) a polyalkene, (ii) a polyester and (iii) a polypeptide.

   (b) Describe briefly how one of the above polymers is manufactured, mentioning the raw materials that are used at the start.

   (c) State, with your reasons, which one of the polymers in (a) you would choose as a suitable material for lining a container for aqueous alkalis, and why the other two are unsuitable. Give for each of the latter an important everyday application.

   (d) Illustrate, with the substances you have chosen in (a) the difference between addition polymerization and condensation polymerization.

3. Explain the chemical nature of the polymers polythene, Terylene and nylon-6 and of the processes involved in their preparation from the appropriate monomers. Is the distinction between addition and condensation polymerization a useful one?

   Account for the general chemical inertness of polythene and indicate what reactions it might be expected to undergo. What bearing does this have on

   (a) the usefulness of polythene and

   (b) the disposal of waste polythene?

   A polymer produced from a benzenedicarboxylic acid and ethane-1,2-diol can be used as a textile fibre; in what ways are the physical properties and uses of the polymer likely to be altered if the ethane-1,2-diol is replaced by propane-1,2,3-triol (glycerol)?

Now that you have an overview of synthetic polymers, we turn to another group of big molecules, namely soaps and detergents. Unlike the substances you have just been studying, these are not polymers.

SOAPS AND DETERGENTS

In this section we consider the structures of soap and detergent molecules and the way in which they act as wetting and grease-removing agents. We start by looking at the formulae of fats, which are the main raw material for soaps.

Objectives.   When you have finished this section you should be able to:

(16)   write a general formula for a fat molecule;

(17)   state the difference between a saturated and an unsaturated fat.

(18)   write down the general structure of a soap (or soapy detergent) and a soapless detergent;

(19)   state the advantages of soapless detergents over soaps;

(20)   explain how soaps and detergents act as wetting and grease-removing agents;

Consult a textbook to find out the general structure of a fat or triglyceride molecule and what happens when it is hydrolysed. Then try the following exercises, which test your understanding of the structure of fats.

Exercise 19   (a)   Explain why fats are often called triglycerides.

(b)   Complete the equation below to show the products of hydrolysis of a generalised fat molecule:

$$CH_2OCOR_1$$
$$|$$
$$CHOCOR_2 \quad + \quad 3NaOH(aq) \quad \rightarrow$$
$$|$$
$$CH_2OCOR_3$$

(Answers on page 86)

As you may already know, sodium salts of long-chain carboxylic acids are the basic ingredients of soaps. The hydrolysis reaction you have just considered is called saponification (Latin: sapo = soap).

In the next exercise you take a look at some of the acids commonly found in fat molecules.

Exercise 20 (a) What is the main difference in physical properties between a saturated and an unsaturated fat?

(b) Table 2 shows the 'shorthand' formulae and melting-points of four long-chain carboxylic acids which occur in fats. We have used the traditional names because the systematic ones are rather clumsy.

Table 2

Long chain carboxylic acid		Melting point/°C
Palmitic	⋀⋀⋀⋀⋀⋀ CO_2H	63
Stearic	⋀⋀⋀⋀⋀⋀⋀ CO_2H	70
Oleic	⋀⋀⋀⋀⋀⋀⋀ CO_2H	16
Linoleic	⋀⋀⋀⋀⋀⋀⋀ CO_2H	-5

Which acids would you expect to be found in higher proportions in unsaturated and saturated fats?

(c) Explain why animal fats have higher melting points than vegetable oils.

(Answers on page 86)

The sodium and potassium salts of these long-chain carboxylic acids (commonly called 'fatty acids') have been used for centuries as soaps to make washing more effective. More recently, with the growth of the petrochemicals industry, synthetic detergents have been developed which are superior in some respects to soap.

Note that, strictly speaking, the class of compounds called 'detergents' includes soaps; to distinguish different types we should use the terms 'soapy detergents' and 'soapless detergents'.

Read about soapless detergents in your textbook(s). Look for their general formulae, noting the difference between anionic and cationic detergents. Also look for their advantages over soap, and the way they work as grease-removing agents and wetting agents. Another important point is the difference between biodegradable and non-biodegradable detergents. You should then be able to do the following exercises.

Exercise 21 (a) Products such as $H_{19}C_9$-⬡-SO_2ONa are extremely useful as detergents.
What advantages do these substances have over soap?

(b) How do the hydrocarbon 'tails' of biodegradable and non-biodegradable detergents differ?

(Answers on page 86)

Exercise 22   Describe the action of detergents

(a) in lowering the surface tension of water,

(b) in the removal of oils and fats.

(Answers on page **87**)

The final exercise in this section is to help you distinguish between anionic and cationic detergents.

Exercise 23   Describe each of the following as either anionic or cationic detergents:

(a) $RSO_2O^-Na^+$ (d) $R-\langle O \rangle - SO_2O^-Na^+$

(b) $RN^+(CH_3)_3Cl^-$

(c) $ROSO_3^-Na^+$ (e) $R_3N^+-\langle O \rangle-Cl^-$

(Answers on page **87**)

Now that you have reached the end of the section on detergents you should look back through your notes and attempt the following Teacher-marked Exercise. Make a plan of your answer first and then spend about 35 minutes writing. Hand both your plan and the answer in to your teacher for marking.

Teacher-marked   What is understood by the word 'detergent'? Explain
       Exercise   in detail the difference in molecular structure
                  between the various types of detergent, both soapy
                  and soapless, and mention the advantages and dis-
                  advantages of each type.

A

LEVEL ONE CHECKLIST

You have now reached the end of Level One of this Unit. Read carefully through the following summary of the objectives in Level One and check that you have adequate notes.

At this stage you should be able to:

(1) show how <u>addition polymers</u> are related to ethene, and write equations for the formation of some examples;

(2) describe a <u>mechanism</u> for the formation of an addition polymer;

(3) distinguish between <u>atactic</u> and <u>isotactic</u> polymers;

(4) quote some examples of <u>condensation polymers</u> and write equations to show their formation;

(5) state the difference between a <u>homopolymer</u> and a <u>copolymer</u>;

(6) & (7) give an example of a <u>cross-linked polymer</u> and describe the effect of cross-linking on physical properties;

(8) & (9) describe how <u>rubber</u> is vulcanized and explain the effect of <u>vulcanization</u> on the properties of rubber;

(10)   explain the meanings of the terms <u>thermosoftening</u> plastic
       (<u>thermoplastic</u>) and <u>thermosetting</u> plastic (<u>thermosett</u>), and
       quote some examples of each;

(11)   list the structural features which increase the <u>crystalline nature</u>
       of polymers;

(12) & (13)   give examples of <u>fibre-forming polymers</u>, stating the structural
              features which favour the formation of fibres;

(14) & (15)   outline the <u>industrial production</u> and <u>principal use(s)</u> of some
              of the following - <u>polyphenylethene</u> (polystyrene), <u>polyethene</u>
              (polythene), low and high density forms, <u>polychloroethene</u>
              (polyvinylchloride, PVC), <u>polytetrafluoroethene</u> (PTFE), <u>nylon</u>,
              <u>Terylene</u>;

(16) & (17)   write a general formula for a <u>fat</u> molecule and state the
              difference between <u>saturated</u> and <u>unsaturated</u> fats;

(18) & (20)   write a generalised structure for a <u>soap</u> (soapy detergent) and
              a <u>soapless detergent</u> and describe how they act as <u>wetting</u> and
              <u>grease-removing agents</u>;

(19)   state the advantages of soapless detergents over soaps.

IN PLACE OF A LEVEL ONE TEST

Instead of a Level One Test, we suggest that you study the photograph below
and try to identify as many different plastics as you can. On page 97 we
have listed 42 items made from 12 different plastics.

However, if you are going to study little or none of Level Two, you should
now attempt questions 1-6 and 24-25 of the End-of-Unit Test which begins on
page 71.

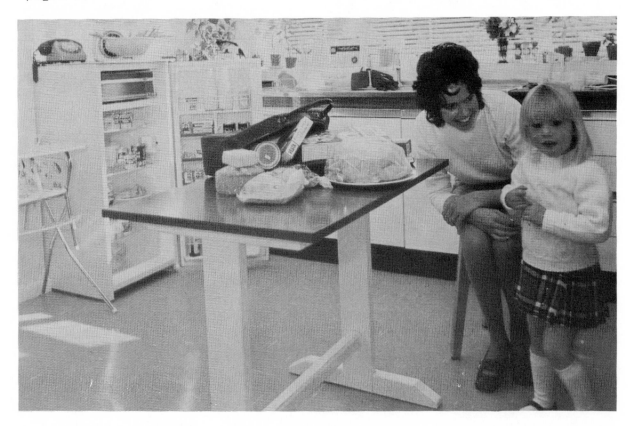

LEVEL TWO

Having looked chiefly at synthetic polymers in Level One, we now turn to natural polymers and big molecules. First we consider proteins and their constituent amino acids, then sugars and, briefly, nucleic acids and lipids.

AMINO ACIDS

Proteins are often called natural polymers but, unlike synthetic ones, they are made up from a selection of about twenty different sub-units, all of which are compounds known as amino acids. Clearly, before you can study proteins, you need to know what amino acids are and how they react.

Formulae of amino acids

In this section you examine the formulae of a number of naturally-occurring amino acids to establish some common features. You also revise some of what you have learned about systematic names.

Objectives. When you have finished this section you should be able to:

(21)   write the general formula for an α-amino acid;

(22)   state the systematic (IUPAC) name for some amino acids;

(23)   recognise an optically-active amino acid from its formula.

Read the introductory section on amino acids in your textbook(s). Look for a generalised formula and find out what are the distinguishing features of naturally-occurring amino acids.

Table 3 on page 26 shows the names and formulae of some of the common amino acids. Don't worry - you need not learn all of these! It will probably be sufficient for you to be able to quote glycine and alanine as examples unless you are studying biochemistry as a special option, in which case your teacher will suggest what else you need to know.

Notice that the trivial names of amino acids, often in an abbreviated three-letter form, are still widely used. In the next exercise, you try naming some amino acids systematically.

Table 3 Naturally-occurring amino-acids

Name & abbreviation		Formula	Name & abbreviation		Formula
Alanine	ala	H_2NCHCO_2H | CH_3	Lysine[4]	lys	H_2NCHCO_2H | $(CH_2)_4$ * | NH_2
Arginine	arg	H_2NCHCO_2H | $(CH_2)_3$ | NH | $HN{=}C{-}NH_2$	Methionine	met	H_2NCHCO_2H | $(CH_2)_2$ | S | CH_3
Aspartic acid[1]	asp	H_2NCHCO_2H | CH_2 | CO_2H	Phenylalanine	phe	H_2NCHCO_2H | CH_2 | ⬡
Cysteine[2]	cys	H_2NCHCO_2H | CH_2 | SH	Proline[5]	pro	$HN{-}CHCO_2H$ ⌐──⌐ *
Glutamic acid[3]	glu	H_2NCHCO_2H | CH_2 | CH_2 | CO_2H	Serine	ser	H_2NCHCO_2H | CH_2OH
Glycine	gly	H_2NCHCO_2H | H	Threonine	thr	H_2NCHCO_2H | $CHOH$ | CH_3
Histidine	his	H_2NCHCO_2H | CH_2 | imidazole (NH, N)	Tryptophan	try	H_2NCHCO_2H | CH_2 | indole (NH)
Isoleucine	ile	H_2NCHCO_2H | $CH{-}CH_3$ | CH_2 | CH_3	Tyrosine	tyr	H_2NCHCO_2H | CH_2 | ⬡ | OH
Leucine	leu	H_2NCHCO_2H | CH_2 | $CH_3{-}CH{-}CH_3$	Valine	val	H_2NCHCO_2H | $CH_3{-}CH{-}CH_3$

1. There is also an amide form called asparagine, asn. ($-CONH_2$ for $-CO_2H$.)
2. Pronounced 'sistane'. Not to be confused with cystine ('sisteen'),
    cys-cys, which consists of 2 cys units linked through the S atoms.
3. There is also an amide form called glutamine, gln. ($-CONH_2$ for $-CO_2H$.)
4. Hydroxylysine has an $-OH$ group substituted in the C_5 position shown.
5. Hydroxyproline has an $-OH$ group substituted in the C_4 position shown.

Exercise 24   (a)   What structural features are common to all the
molecules shown in Table 3?

(b)   What is the significance of the letter α in the
title α-amino acid?

(c)   Write systematic names for:

(i)   glycine,   (iii)   serine,   (v)   lysine,

(ii)   alanine,   (iv)   phenylalanine,   (vi)   valine.

(d)   Why are systematic names not often used for amino acids?

(e)   Which of the amino acids in Table 3 would you <u>not</u> expect
to be optically active?

(Answers on page **87**)

We now consider the behaviour of amino acids, beginning with physical
properties and acid-base character.

Physical properties and acid-base behaviour of amino acids

<u>Objectives</u>.   When you have finished this section you should be able to:

(24)   explain how the <u>physical properties of amino acids</u> provide evidence
for the existence of <u>zwitterions</u>;

(25)   write equations for the <u>reactions of an amino acid</u> with acids and
alkalis;

(26)   distinguish between <u>acidic</u>, <u>basic</u> and <u>neutral amino acids</u>;

(27)   explain the term <u>isoelectric point</u> and show how amino acid solutions
act as <u>buffers</u>.

Before you start work on this section, you may need to read through
your notes from Units 02, 03 and P3 to revise the reactions of amino
and carboxyl groups and the properties of buffer solutions.   Also
read about the physical properties of amino acids, looking for an
explanation of the term 'zwitterion' (or '<u>dipolar ion</u>').   This will
enable you to do the next exercise.

Exercise 25   Why does glycine have such a high melting-point compared
with the compounds of similar molar mass listed in the
table below?

Table 4

Compound	Molar mass/g mol^{-1}	Melting-point/°C
Glycine	75	235
Propanoic acid	74	-21
Methyl ethanoate	74.1	-98
1-aminobutane	73.1	-49

(Answer on page **87**)

27

Amino acids are bifunctional compounds containing both amino and carboxyl groups. We would therefore expect them to react with both acids and alkalis, an idea which you explore in the next exercise.

Exercise 26   Write equations to show how you would expect a molecule of alanine, in the form $CH_3CH(NH_2)CO_2H$, to react with:

(a) dilute aqueous sodium hydroxide,

(b) dilute hydrochloric acid.

(Answers on page 87)

When an amino acid is dissolved in water, a series of equilibria is set up, as you find out in the next exercise.

Exercise 27   The equations below show the equilibria which are set up when the amino acid glycine is in solution:

$$H_2N-CH_2-CO_2^- \rightleftharpoons H_3N^+-CH_2-CO_2^- \rightleftharpoons H_3N^+-CH_2-CO_2H$$

A $\pm H^+$ B $\pm H^+$ C

(a) Which of the forms A, B and C would you expect to be in greatest concentration at low pH and at high pH? Explain.

(b) Describe the forms A, B and C using the terms conjugate acid, conjugate base and zwitterion.

(c) Which of the three forms do you think would show no net movement in an electric field?

(Answers on page 87)

The pH at which the zwitterion form is at maximum concentration is the isoelectric point or isoelectric pH. At this pH, an amino acid possesses no net charge and does not migrate in an electric field. This is useful in the separation and identification of amino acids, as you will see later. In the next exercise, you explore the range of isoelectric points.

Exercise 28   (a) By examining the formulae of the amino acids shown below, classify them as acidic, basic or neutral.

(b) Is there a relation between isoelectric pH and the type of amino acid?

Table 5

Amino acid	Formula	Isoelectric pH
Arginine	$HN=C(NH_2)NH(CH_2)_3CH(NH_2)CO_2H$	10.8
Aspartic acid	$CO_2HCH_2CH(NH_2)CO_2H$	2.8
Glutamic acid	$CO_2H(CH_2)_2CH(NH_2)CO_2H$	3.2
Glycine	$CH_2(NH_2)CO_2H$	6.0
Leucine	$(CH_3)_2CHCH_2CH(NH_2)CO_2H$	6.0
Lysine	$H_2N(CH_2)_4CH(NH_2)CO_2H$	10.0

(Answers on page 88)

In the next exercise you apply your knowledge of the ionization of amino acids to see how they can act as buffer solutions. You may need to revise the expression you first met in Unit P3 (Equilibrium II: Acids and Bases):

$$pH = pK_a - \log \frac{[acid]}{[base]}$$

Exercise 29 Fig. 10 is a titration curve for glycine. (The shape may seem unfamiliar to you because pH is shown here along the x-axis, not the y-axis as in Unit P3.)

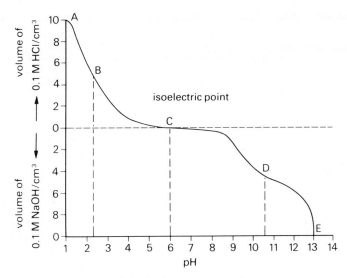

Fig. 10. Titration curve for 0.001 mol of glycine

(a) Use formulae to show which form of glycine would predominate at points A, C and E in Fig. 10.

(b) The pK_a values for glycine are $pK_1 = 2.34$, $pK_2 = 9.60$ Use these to decide the species and the ratio in which they are present at points B and D on the graph.

(c) Over which ranges of pH does glycine behave as (i) a good buffer, and (ii) a poor buffer? Explain.

(Answers on page **88**)

The next exercise consists of parts of two A-level questions.

Exercise 30 (a) 2-aminopropanoic acid, (alanine), has pK_a values of 2.4 and 9.7 at 298 K. Discuss the species present at different pH values when aqueous solutions of alanine at pH = 7 are titrated with:

    (i) hydrochloric acid to a pH of 1.5,

    (ii) aqueous sodium hydroxide to a pH of 11.5.

(b) State what species you think will be present in similar titrations using 2,6-diaminohexanoic acid, (lysine), the pK_a values being 2.2, 9.0 and 10.5.

(c) The pK_a values for aspartic acid, $CO_2HCH_2CH(NH_2)CO_2H$, are 2.1, 3.9 and 9.8. From your knowledge of the acid-base behaviour of amino acids, give the structures of the species which predominate in a solution of aspartic acid at pH = 1, 7 and 13.

(Answers on page **88**)

Now we move on to consider some further reactions of amino acids.

Chemical reactions of amino acids

Most of these reactions are what you would expect from your knowledge of the two functional groups.

Objectives. When you have finished this section you should be able to:

(28)   state how an amino acid reacts with nitrous acid, ethanol, ethanoic anhydride and soda-lime;

(29)   describe the reaction between aqueous glycine and copper(II) ions.

Read about the chemical reactions of amino acids, comparing them with what you already know about amino compounds and carboxylic acids. You should then be able to do the following exercises.

Exercise 31   (a) Write an equation for the reaction between alanine and nitrous acid.

(b)   (i) Which reagents could you use to acylate alanine? (Acylation is the substitution of RC=O for H.)

(ii) Write an equation to show acylation using one of these reagents.

(c)   (i) Write an equation for the esterification reaction between alanine and ethanol.

(ii) How is this reaction catalysed?

(Answers on page 89)

Exercise 32   Use the information below to identify, by name and formula, substances G, H and I.

G is a crystalline solid which has a high melting-point (over 200 °C) and dissolves in water to give an almost neutral solution. It forms crystalline salts with both acids and bases, and yields a pungent-smelling gas, H, when heated with soda-lime. H burns in air and dissolves in water to give an alkaline solution. When G is treated with nitrous acid it yields nitrogen, water and an acid I with a relative molecular mass of 76.

(Answers on page 89)

Before you do the next exercise, which is about the complex formed between glycine in solution and copper(II) ions, we suggest a short experiment which should take you no more than ten minutes.

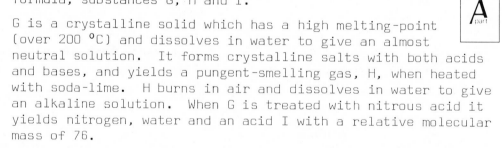

EXPERIMENT 1

The glycine/copper(II) complex

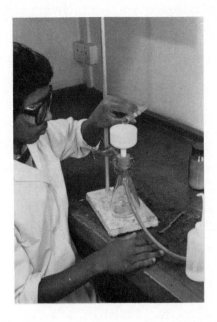

Aim and Introduction

The purpose of this simple experiment is to prepare a complex from glycine and copper(II) ions.

Requirements

safety spectacles
wash-bottle of distilled water
test-tube
spatula
glycine, $CH_2NH_2CO_2H$
copper(II) carbonate, $CuCO_3$ (powdered)
stirring rod
Büchner funnel (small) or Hirsch funnel
filter paper
filter tube with side-arm
filter pump and pressure tubing
crystallizing dish

Procedure

1. To about 10 cm^3 of distilled water in a test-tube, add about 0.5 g (small spatula measure) of glycine. Note how easily it dissolves.

2. Slowly add powdered copper(II) carbonate, stirring the contents of the tube between additions. Keep adding the powder until it is in excess.

3. Set up a small Büchner funnel or Hirsch funnel in a side-arm filter tube.

4. Transfer the filtrate to a crystallizing dish and allow it to stand. Note the colour of the solution and whether crystals are formed.

Questions

1. Copper(II) carbonate is only slightly soluble but during the experiment some CO_3^{2-} ions do dissolve. Would you expect this to make the solution slightly acidic, neutral or alkaline? Explain.

2. Bearing in mind your answer to Question 1, what form of glycine would you expect to predominate in the solution?

3. How many bonds is each glycine molecule capable of making with Cu^{2+}(aq) under these conditions?

(Answers on page 89)

Exercise 33 (a) Bearing in mind your answers to the questions following Experiment 1 and your knowledge of the types of complex formed by copper(II) ions, suggest a structural formula for the copper(II)/glycine complex.

(b) What shape and charge would this complex have?

(Answers on page 89)

Having looked at the properties of amino acids, we now turn to methods of preparation.

Preparation of amino acids

There are two main methods for preparing amino acids. Each uses the reactions of functional groups which you have already studied.

<u>Objective</u>. When you have finished this section you should be able to:

(30) outline two general methods for the <u>preparation of amino acids</u>.

Read about the methods for making amino acids from aldehydes and via the chlorination of alkanoic acids. You may find one of these methods listed as the <u>Strecker synthesis.</u> This should enable you to do the next exercise.

<u>Exercise 34</u>
(a) Show how aminoethanoic acid (glycine) may be prepared, in three stages, from ethanoic acid.

(b) Show how 2-aminopropanoic acid (alanine) may be prepared from ethanal.

(c) Would you expect the products from (a) and (b) to be optically active?

(Answers on page **90**)

To help consolidate your knowledge of the reactions of amino acids, you should now attempt the following Teacher-marked Exercise, which is an A-level essay-style question. Before you attempt the question, look back through your notes and make a plan of the points you think your answer should include. Spend about 40 minutes on both your plan and your answer.

<u>Teacher-marked</u>
<u>Exercise</u>
Amino acids contain two different functional groups in the same molecule. Describe some typical physical and chemical properties of this class of compound and, where possible, interpret these properties in terms of the structure possessed by amino acids.

The reactions you have considered so far do not suggest that amino acids might polymerize. However, in biological systems, amino acids do link together to form compounds called peptides, polypeptides and proteins. We consider the way in which proteins are built up from amino acids in the next section.

PROTEINS

In biological systems, the $-NH_2$ group from one amino acid molecule is enabled to react with the $-CO_2H$ group in another molecule (or in a growing chain) by the action of a specific enzyme catalyst. Many series of such reactions, involving twenty-odd different amino acids, result in the formation of proteins, which form a large proportion of animal tissue.

In laboratory conditions it is much easier to split up proteins than it is to synthesise them. In this section, you see how the hydrolysis of proteins enables us to work out both the identity of the constituent amino acids and the order in which they are linked together. First, however, we look at the nature of the linkage between amino acid molecules.

The peptide link

Objectives. When you have finished this section you should be able to:

(31) write a generalised equation for the formation of a peptide link between two amino acids;

(32) explain why amino acids do not readily form peptide links in ordinary conditions;

(33) explain the terms dipeptide, tripeptide and polypeptide.

Read about the peptide link in order to help you with the next exercise.

Exercise 35 (a) Write an equation to show a condensation reaction between the $-NH_2$ group in one molecule of alanine and the $-CO_2H$ group in another.

(b) From what you know of the acid-base nature of alanine, why do you think the reaction in (a) does not occur readily in aqueous solution?

(c) How can the alanine molecule be modified so that a similar condensation reaction does readily occur, giving the same product as in (a)?

(d) The product of the reaction is called alanylalanine. Why is this name used in preference to a systematic name? What type of compound is it?

(Answers on page 90)

You saw in the last exercise that it is a fairly simple matter to make a dipeptide from a single amino acid, and this dipeptide could react further in the same way to form a tripeptide and a polypeptide. This polypeptide is not, of course, a protein because it is built up from only one amino acid.

It is not so simple to make a dipeptide from two different amino acids, A and B. In order to prevent identical molecules from combining together, the $-NH_2$ group in A and the $-CO_2H$ group in B must be protected in some way. Ask your teacher whether you should find out how this is done by reading a suitable textbook.

The mechanism of protein synthesis in biological systems is too complex for A-level study. Instead we turn directly to the structure of proteins.

STRUCTURE OF PROTEINS

Early workers used the powerful technique of X-ray diffraction to unravel protein structures. We deal with the basic principles of X-ray diffraction in Appendix 1 at the end of this unit. Check with your teacher whether you need to know this for your particular syllabus.

Objectives. When you have finished this section you should be able to:

(34) distinguish between a fibrous and a globular protein;

(35) explain how restricted rotation around the peptide bond gives it a planar shape;

(36) distinguish between the primary, secondary and tertiary structures of a protein;

(37) state and explain the roles of the peptide bond, hydrogen bonding, and disulphide bridges in protein structure;

(38) explain what happens when a protein denatures.

Start by reading about protein structure in a textbook. Many books classify proteins according to their biological functions, as fibrous and globular. Try to find out the structural difference between these two types. Also look for an explanation of primary, secondary and tertiary structures in proteins.

Primary structures

You have already seen that a protein molecule is a long chain consisting of amino acid units joined together by peptide links. The sequence of amino acid units (sometimes called residues) is the primary structure of a protein.

The importance of this sequence of amino acid units is illustrated by the 'molecular disease' known as sickle-cell anaemia. People suffering from this disorder have a proportion of sickle-shaped red blood cells, which absorb oxygen less efficiently than the normal disc-shaped cells (see Fig. 11).

This vital difference in function has been shown to be due to the misplacement of only <u>one</u> of the 574 amino acid units in the protein haemoglobin!

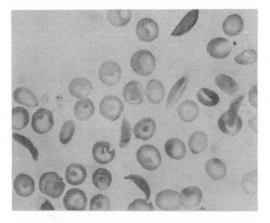

Fig. 11.   Normal (disc-shaped) and sickle red blood cells

Before we look at the methods by which primary structures have been determined, we consider the factors which control the shapes adopted by the long protein chains.

Secondary structure

The nature of the peptide link affects the shape of a protein molecule, as you see in the next exercise.

Exercise 36   Fig. 12 shows the average bond lengths for a typical peptide link.

Average bond lengths for C—N and C≡N are 0.147 nm and 0.127 nm respectively.

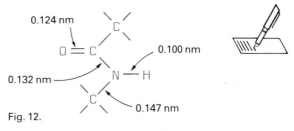

Fig. 12.

(a)   Using this information, comment on the nature of the central C—N bond in a peptide link.

(b)   Explain how the nature of this central C—N bond makes the peptide link planar.

(c)   On a sketch outline the area which is approximately planar.

(Answers on page 90)

The planar peptide link has the effect of restricting the rotation at every third bond in the polypeptide chain, as shown in Fig. 13.

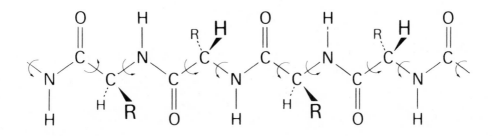

Fig. 13.

35

The limited rotation about the peptide links is one factor which affects the shape of the protein molecules. The most important factor, however, is the possibility of hydrogen bonding at various points within each molecule if the chain folds back on itself.

The dimensions of the —N—C—C—N—C—C—N—C—C—N— skeleton are common to all proteins and, consequently, similar secondary structures are found in different proteins. The two most important are the β-pleated-sheet and the α-helix, illustrated in Figs. 14 and 15. In each case, large numbers of hydrogen bonds hold the different parts of the chain in fixed positions.

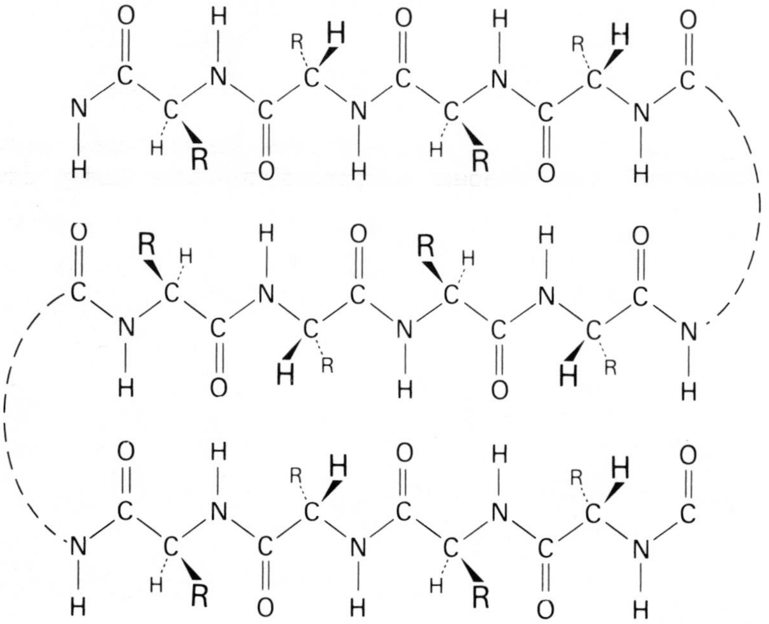

Fig. 14.   β-pleated-sheet structure of a protein

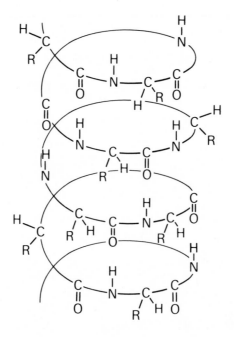

Fig. 15.   α-helix structure of a protein

The next exercise concerns Figs. 14 and 15.

Exercise 37 (a) On a photocopy of Figs. 14 and 15, sketch in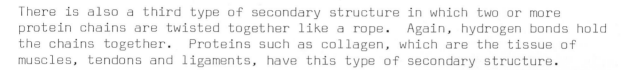

        (i)   the hydrogen bonds,

        (ii) The planar regions around the peptide links.

   (b) How would you describe the position of the R groups, relative to the peptide links in each structure?

(Answers on page **90**)

There is also a third type of secondary structure in which two or more protein chains are twisted together like a rope. Again, hydrogen bonds hold the chains together. Proteins such as collagen, which are the tissue of muscles, tendons and ligaments, have this type of secondary structure.

The nature of the R groups attached to the —N—C—C—N—C—C—N— skeleton decides which type of secondary structure is adopted by a particular protein. However, some proteins change from one structure to another in different conditions. For instance, keratin, the protein in hair, usually exists as α-helices but, when it is stretched or in contact with hot water, it forms β-pleated-sheets. This is why your hair gets shorter and springier when you dry it.

Fibrous proteins, such as those in hair, silk, wool, etc., contain relatively few different amino acids, and these are arranged in regularly-repeating units. Consequently, the same secondary structure is repeated throughout. In more complicated proteins, parts of the chain may be helical, but the secondary structure is folded back on itself to give a convoluted globular shape - hence the name globular proteins. We discuss an example in the next section.

Tertiary structure

The folding of the polymer chain in globular proteins was once thought to be random, but X-ray diffraction has shown that each one has a definite structure. The complex folding produces reactive sites of precise dimensions to enable specific reactions to occur. For example, certain enzymes are able to promote the formation of peptide links in protein synthesis, as shown diagrammatically in Fig. 16.

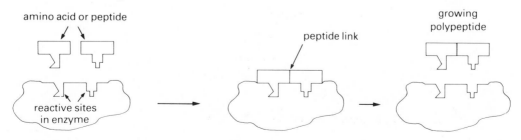

Fig. 16.   Formation of a peptide link catalysed by an enzyme

Once again, hydrogen bonding contributes to tertiary structure. Other factors are ionic bonding between acidic and basic amino acids, and sulphur bridging between cysteine units. This bridging is sometimes regarded as part of the primary structure, with cys-cys (cystine) being regarded as a single amino acid. (See Table 3 on page 26.)

In the next exercise you explore the tertiary structure of lysozyme with the help of Figs. 17 and 18 below. Fig. 17 shows the primary structure giving the amino acid sequence, and Fig. 18 gives an indication of the secondary and tertiary structures. You may also need your textbook.

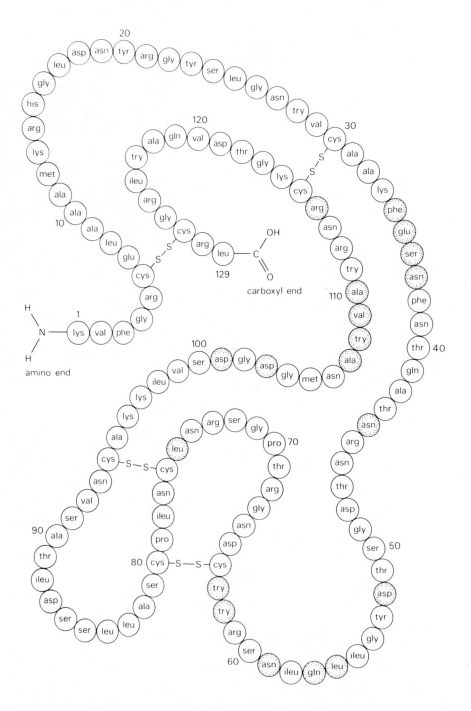

Fig. 17. Primary structure of lysozyme

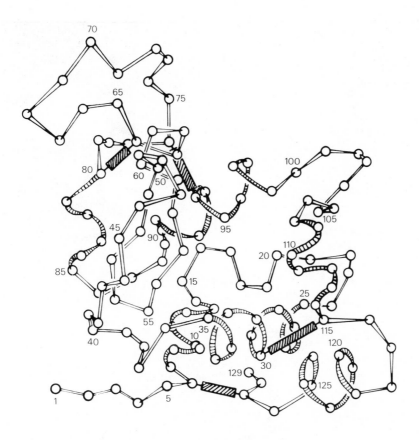

Fig. 18. Secondary and tertiary structure of lysozyme

Exercise 38   (a)   On Fig. 18, trace along the outline of the protein
chain starting at the amino end, residue 1. List
the amino acid residue numbers of the areas which
show α-helical secondary structure.

(b)   The chain is held together in four places by disulphide
bridges.

(i)   State which amino acid forms disulphide bridges.

(ii)   Write an equation for the reaction in which a
disulphide bridge is formed. (Assume that the amino
and carboxyl group of each amino acid are involved in
peptide bonds.)

(iii)   What type of reaction is this?

(c)   In addition to hydrogen bonding, another type of bonding
can operate between certain amino acid residues. Write an
equation to show the formation of such a bond between
glutamic acid and lysine residues.

(d)   What happens to the structure of lysozyme when it is
'denatured' and how may this be achieved?

(Answers on page 91)

We end this section of work on protein structure with a very short
experiment which enables you to detect the presence of a protein in
an aqueous mixture.

39

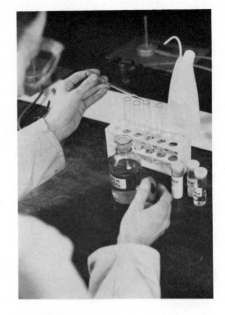

EXPERIMENT 2
Biuret test for proteins

Aim

This experiment is intended to give you practical experience of the biuret test for proteins.

Introduction

The biuret test is based on a coloured complex formed between copper(II) ions and the peptide links of neighbouring protein chains. You carry out the test on examples of available protein material.

Requirements

safety spectacles
4 test-tubes in a rack
spatula
protein sample(s) (e.g. egg albumin, gelatin, fresh milk)
wash-bottle of distilled water
sodium hydroxide solution, 2 M NaOH — — — — — — — — — — — — — — — — — —
teat-pipette
copper(II) sulphate solution, 0.1 M CuSO$_4$

Procedure

1. Take a small amount (enough to cover a spatula tip if solid, about 2 cm^3 in the bottom of a test-tube, if liquid) of one of the proteins. Dissolve it in water so that the total volume is no more than $\frac{1}{4}$ of a test-tube. If necessary, warm the tube.

2. Allow the contents of the tube to cool.

3. Add an equal volume of 2 M sodium hydroxide solution followed by 5 drops of 0.1 M copper(II) sulphate solution.

4. Leave the tube to stand, if necessary, and note the colour that develops.

5. Repeat steps 3 and 4 using water instead of protein solution. Compare the colour of this 'blank' tube with the colour of your protein solution from 3. If you don't get a definite colour, try again with a more concentrated protein solution in step 1.

6. Repeat steps 1 to 4 using other protein(s).

1. How do you think the biuret test might be used to estimate the concentration of a protein in a solution?

2. The biuret test is named after the compound:

$$H_2N-\underset{\underset{O}{\|}}{C}-NH-\underset{\underset{O}{\|}}{C}-NH_2$$
biuret

Given the fact that the Cu^{2+} ion forms 4-coordinate, planar complexes, suggest a possible formula for the complex between Cu^{2+} and two protein chains.

3. If you hydrolysed a protein sample and converted it completely into its constituent amino acids, would you expect to get a positive biuret test? Explain.

(Answers on page 91)

We referred to X-ray crystallography at several points in the last section as a method of structure determination. In the next section we look at the chemical methods, amino acid analysis and sequence determination, which are used to complement X-ray analysis.

Determining the primary structure of a protein

It is relatively easy to hydrolyse a protein completely into separate amino acids which can be identified by chromatography; you learn about the technique in Experiment 3 later in this Unit. However, working out the order in which the amino acids are joined together is much more difficult - a kind of chemical jigsaw puzzle.

A technique for the sequence determination of amino acids in a protein chain was worked out over several years by Sanger in the 1920s. Additional methods have now allowed the processes to be automated so that what once took months (even years) can now be done in hours.

Objectives. When you have finished this section you should be able to:

(39) state the reaction of 1-fluoro-2,4-dinitrobenzene (FDNB) with an amino acid;

(40) explain what is meant by the 'N-terminal' and 'C-terminal' ends of a polypeptide chain;

(41) explain the role of enzymes such as trypsin and carboxypeptidase in sequence determination;

(42) explain how N-terminal analysis of a polypeptide is carried out.

Read about sequence determination in a polypeptide. You may find this listed in the index under <u>Sanger</u>. Look for an account of the way in which partial hydrolysis of a protein can be controlled. For a reasonably full description you may have to use an organic chemistry textbook (rather than a general one) or a simple biochemistry book.

One of Sanger's techniques concerned the reaction between 1-fluoro-2,4-dinitrobenzene and an amino group. You explore this reaction in the next exercise.

Exercise 39   (a)   Write the formula for 1-fluoro-2,4-dinitrobenzene.

               (b)   Give an equation to show how FDNB reacts with alanine, $CH_3CH(NH_2)CO_2H$.

               (c)   The bond between FDNB and an amino acid is resistant to hydrolysis. In what way would this be useful in the sequence determination of a polypeptide?

(Answers on page 91)

Another technique used in sequence determination is to digest a peptide with carboxypeptidase for about twelve hours. This enzyme releases amino acids, sequentially, from the C-terminal end of the peptide. You have probably met the technique in your reading. We include an example in the following exercises.

Exercise 40   A pentapeptide was isolated from a certain bacterium. Several tests were carried out on the pentapeptide and their results are given below. Use the information to suggest a sequence for the amino acids in the peptide.

               (a)   On total hydrolysis, the following amino acids were identified, in the given proportions:

                    arginine (1), glycine (2), lysine (1), valine (1).

               (b)   On partial hydrolysis, the following dipeptides were identified: gly-gly, val-gly; lys-val; gly-arg.

               (c)   1.00 g of the pentapeptide, whose relative molecular mass is 501, was treated with carboxypeptidase for twelve hours. The amino acids released were:

                    arginine: 2.1×10^{-3} mol   glycine: 4.3×10^{-3} mol

               (d)   The pentapeptide was treated with 1-fluoro-2,4-dinitrobenzene (FDNB). After hydrolysis DNP-lysine was identified by chromatography.

(Answers on page 91)

Exercise 41   The amino acid sequence in a peptide can, in favourable
              circumstances, be determined from the amino acids formed
              on hydrolysis and the dipeptides formed on partial
              hydrolysis. A certain tetrapeptide on hydrolysis gave
              alanine and glycine in the molecular ratio of 3:1. Describe
              how such a result can be established. On partial hydrolysis,
              the only dipeptides formed were glycylalanine and alanylalanine.
              Describe how the structures of these dipeptides can be
              established experimentally. Suggest a structure for the
              tetrapeptide.

┌───┐
│ A │
└───┘

              (Answer on page **91**)

We now return to examine the technique of paper chromatography, which has
played a vital part in the determination of primary structure.

Chromatography

All chromatographic methods depend on similar principles. In this section
we concentrate on paper chromatography, but you may also need to be able to
outline other techniques such as thin-layer chromatography (TLC), electro-
phoresis, column chromatography and gas-liquid chromatography (GLC). Ask
your teacher how much you should study.

Objectives. When you have finished this section you should be able to:

(43)   outline the role of chromatography in the determination of the primary
       structure of a protein;

(44)   explain the terms stationary and mobile phase, eluent and adsorbant,
       adsorption and partition, in the context of chromatography;

(45)   outline the distinguishing features of four types of chromatography -
       column, thin-layer, paper and gas-liquid;

(46)   explain the difference between ascending and descending chromatography;

(47)   explain the use of ninhydrin solution in detecting amino acids on
       chromatograms;

(48)   explain what an R_f value is and calculate such values for substances
       on a paper chromatogram;

(49)   carry out a simple separation of amino acids using paper chromatography.

Find a textbook which has a section on chromatography. As the
technique is more important in organic chemistry, you should find a
more detailed treatment in a separate organic textbook. Scan the
whole section, including column, thin-layer, paper and gas-liquid
chromatography. You need to identify the principle behind each
method as well as the substances used in it and the main factors
affecting the process.

You should now do the next exercise, which is to help you summarise
and record what you have learned from your reading.

Exercise 42 (a) Complete a copy of the following table to show the characteristics of the four main types of chromatography

Table 6

Type of chromatography	Separation phases		Principle - adsorption or partition
	Mobile	Stationary	
Column	Liquid	Solid	Adsorption*
Thin-layer			
Paper			
Gas-liquid			

*Partition between eluent and adsorbed liquid may be important in some cases.

(b) Which substances are commonly used on the stationary phase in column and thin-layer chromatography?

(c) In column chromatography, the substances making up the stationary phase are usually used in an 'activated' form.

   (i) Explain what happens when these substances are activated.

   (ii) How does the activated form affect the progress of a substance in a chromatography column?

(d) What are the main factors affecting the rate at which substances separate?

(Answers on page 92)

We do not discuss gas-liquid chromatography further in this Unit. However, if it is available, you may wish to see part of the ILPAC video-programme. 'Instrumental Techniques', which illustrates the procedure.

Now you can gain some practical experience of chromatography. We have chosen a method using paper because it lends itself to a simple and quick experiment although, as you have learned from your reading, the other types of chromatography are now of more importance. However, you can apply your knowledge of paper chromatography to the other techniques if you need to study them as well.

If it is available, watch the ILPAC video-programme 'Organic Techniques 3', in which we demonstrate paper chromatography and explain the calculation of R_f values.

If you are unable to watch the video-programme, read about R_f values in a suitable textbook and make sure you know how to calculate them.

44

Aim

The purpose of this experiment is to
illustrate the use of paper chromatography
for the separation and identification of
amino acids.

Introduction

In this experiment you separate a mixture of three amino acids by means of
paper chromatography. From the chromatogram you calculate R_f values for the
individual amino acids.

Requirements

safety spectacles and protective gloves
measuring cylinder, 10 cm³
beaker, 400 cm³, tall-form
watch glass (big enough to cover beaker)
ethanol, C_2H_5OH
wash-bottle of distilled water
ammonia solution, 0.880 NH_3- – – – – – – – – – – – – – – – – – –
square of chromatography paper, 12.5 cm x 12.5 cm
pencil and ruler
4 melting-point tubes
aspartic acid solution, 0.01 M
leucine solution, 0.01 M
lysine solution, 0.01 M
mixture of the three amino acids above
2 retort stands, bosses and clamps
2 paper clips
hair-dryer
ninhydrin aerosol spray –
oven (105 °C)

Hazard warning

Concentrated ammonia solution is corrosive and gives off harmful
vapour. Therefore you MUST:

WEAR SAFETY SPECTACLES AND GLOVES
KEEP BOTTLES CLOSED AS MUCH AS POSSIBLE

Ninhydrin sprays give off toxic fumes. Therefore you MUST:

WORK AT A FUME CUPBOARD
READ THE INSTRUCTIONS ON THE AEROSOL CAN

---

1. In a fume cupboard, prepare the solvent mixture by pouring the following into a 400 cm³ tall-form beaker:

    24 cm³ of ethanol,
     3 cm³ of distilled water,
     3 cm³ of 0.880 ammonia.

2. Cover the beaker with a watch-glass. Swirl to mix the liquids and leave to stand.

3. Handling it only by the top edge, place a square of chromatography paper on a clean sheet of file paper. With a pencil (not a pen) draw lines and labels as shown in Fig. 19.

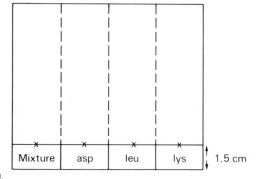

Fig. 19.

4. Dip a clean melting-point tube into the solution of mixed amino acids and then touch it briefly on the appropriate labelled cross so that a spot, no more than 5 mm across, appears on the paper.

5. Using a fresh tube each time, repeat step 4 for each of the three solutions of single amino acids.

6. Place a clean ruler with its edge along one of the dashed lines and hold it firmly in place with one hand. Without touching it with your fingers, fold the chromatography paper along the line by sliding your hand under the file paper and lifting.

7. Repeat the folding procedure for the other two lines so that the opposite edges of the paper almost meet to form a square cross-section.

8. Hold the paper by the edge furthest from the start line, and place it in the beaker so that it does not touch the sides. Replace the cover and leave to stand.

9. Clamp the ruler horizontally at a height of 20-30 cm between two retort stands in a fume-cupboard. This is to support the chromatography paper for drying when the run has finished.

10. While you are waiting, get on with some other work, but look at the paper every 10 minutes to see how far the solvent has soaked up the paper.

11. When the solvent has reached nearly to the top of the paper (30-40 minutes) or when you have only 15 minutes laboratory time left, whichever is the sooner, remove the paper from the beaker, open it out and clip it on to the ruler to dry. You can hasten the drying with a hair-dryer.

12. When the paper is dry, spray it evenly with ninhydrin solution. Dry it again and then heat it in an oven at 105 °C for 5 minutes.

13. Remove the paper from the oven and mark with a pencil the positions of the coloured spots.

14. Measure the distances from the origin line to the centres of the spots and record them in a copy of Results Table 3.

Results and calculations

Calculate an R_f value for each spot as follows:

$$R_f = \frac{\text{distance travelled by spot}}{\text{distance travelled by solvent}}$$

Results Table 3

| Amino acid | Distances travelled/cm | | R_f value |
	by solvent	by amino acid	
Aspartic acid - alone - in mixture			
Leucine - alone - in mixture			
Lysine - alone - in mixture			

(Specimen results on page 92)

Questions

1. For each amino acid, compare your two R_f values with each other and with our specimen results. Why do you think there is some variation?

2. Why do R_f values change when a different solvent is used?

3. Why is it so important to avoid touching the chromatography paper with your fingers?

(Answers on page 92)

A protein hydrolysate may contain as many as twenty different amino acids and it is not possible to separate all of them completely by the simple method you have just used. Whichever solvent is chosen, there is always at least one pair of amino acids with almost identical R_f values.

To overcome this problem, two-way paper chromatography was developed. A single spot of mixture is placed in one corner of the paper and is partially separated by one solvent in the usual way into a line of spots, some of which contain more than one amino acid. The paper is then dried, turned through 90° and placed in a solvent of different character from the first. The solvents are chosen so that no two amino acids have the same R_f values in both; this means that a complete separation can be done on a complex mixture.

It is notoriously difficult to obtain reproducible results using paper chromatography - R_f values can vary widely from one experiment to another. For this reason, two-way chromatography is more often done on glass plates covered with a layer of solid adsorbant, but the general appearance of the chromatograms, and the calculation of R_f values, are much the same.

The next exercise tests your understanding of two-way chromatography.

Exercise 43   The table below gives data about a number of amino acids which occur in proteins.

Table 7

Name and abbreviation		Relative molecular mass	R_f value in phenol	R_f value in butan-1-ol acetic acid
Alanine	ala	89	0.43	0.38
Aspartic acid	asp	133	0.13	0.24
Glycine	gly	75	0.33	0.26
Leucine	leu	131	0.66	0.73
Lysine	lys	146	0.62	0.14
Phenylalanine	phe	165	0.64	0.68
Serine	ser	105	0.30	0.27
Valine	val	117	0.58	0.40

A small polypeptide was hydrolyzed with 6 M acid and the resulting amino acids were separated by two-way chromatography. The chromatogram is reproduced below.

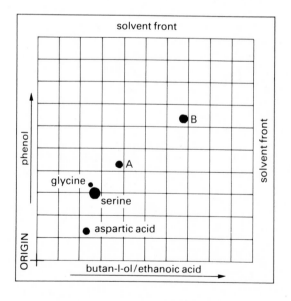

Fig. 20.

<u>Exercise 43</u>   (continued)

(a) Determine the R_f values in both solvents of the amino acids labelled A and B on the chromatogram, and identify them.

(b) The polypeptide was reacted with 1-fluoro-2,4-dinitro-benzene (FDNB). After hydrolysis, DNP-glycine was identified by chromatography. What information does this give about the sequence of amino acids in the polypeptide?

(c) When 1.00 g of the polypeptide, whose molar mass was found to be about 780 g mol^{-1}, was subjected to the action of carboxypeptidase for twelve hours, the amino acids released were:

serine	2.5×10^{-3} mol
aspartic acid	1.2×10^{-3} mol
amino acid	1.1×10^{-3} mol

What information does this result give about the sequence of amino acids in the polypeptide?

(d) Quantitative estimation of the amino acids in the polypeptide showed that they were present in the following molar ratio:

serine	3
aspartic acid	2
amino acid A	1
amino acid B	1
glycine	1

Using this information and information from the previous sections, which of the following is the most probable sequence of amino acids in the polypeptide?

(i)   (NH$_2$)-gly-ser-B-asp-ser-asp-A-(CO$_2$H)

(ii) (NH$_2$)-gly-asp-A-ser-B-asp-ser-ser-(CO$_2$H)

(iii) (NH$_2$)-gly-ser-B-asp-A-asp-ser-ser-(CO$_2$H)

(iv) (NH$_2$)-ser-ser-asp-A-ser-B-asp-gly-(CO$_2$H)

(v)   (NH$_2$)-A-asp-ser-ser-ser-B-asp-gly-(CO$_2$H)

What is the correct sequence?

Explain your reasoning for each of the sequences (i) to (v).

(Answers on page 92)

The next exercise takes the form of five multiple-choice questions based on a practical situation.

Questions 1-5 refer to the experiment described below.
Select the best answer for each question.

In order to determine which acid in a mixed dipeptide has
a free amino group, these procedures are adopted.

  (i)   The dipeptide, dissolved in sodium hydrogencarbonate
        solution, is warmed with excess 1-fluoro-2,4-dinitro-
        benzene dissolved in ethanol, to give a nitrophenyl
        peptide.

  (ii) The mixture is then extracted with ether.

  (iii) The aqueous layer is heated with a little concentrated
        hydrochloric acid.

  (iv) A second ether extraction is carried out, the ether
        removed and the residue from the ether extract examined
        chromatographically.

$$NO_2 \text{—} F \quad + \quad H_2NCHR^1CONHCHR^2CO_2H$$

$$O_2N$$

NaHCO$_3$(aq)
at 40 °C

$$NO_2 \text{—} NHCHR^1CONHCHR^2CO_2H$$

$$O_2N$$

Acid hydrolysis
at 100 °C

$$NO_2 \text{—} NHCHR^1CO_2H \quad + \quad H_2NCHR^2CO_2H$$

$$O_2N$$

1. The purpose of the first ether extraction is to remove:

   A fluoride ions   D unchanged dipeptide

   B sodium hydrogencarbonate   E unchanged 1-fluoro-2,4-
                                        dinitrobenzene
   C alcohol

2. The second amino acid ($H_2NCHR^2CO_2H$) from the dipeptide

   A dissolves in the ether in the first ether extraction,

   B dissolves in the ether in the second ether extraction,

   C is destroyed in the acid hydrolysis,

   D remains in the aqueous layer after the second ether
      extraction

   E forms a fluoro-derivative with the fluoride ions.

3. A number of yellow spots appeared on the chromatogram. Which one corresponds to a dinitrophenyl amino acid with an R_f value of 0.30-0.35?

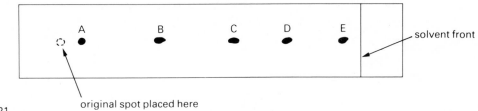

Fig. 21.

original spot placed here

4. A student found four other yellow spots on the chromatogram in addition to the dinitrophenyl amino acid. Which of the follow compounds would be LEAST likely to be present?

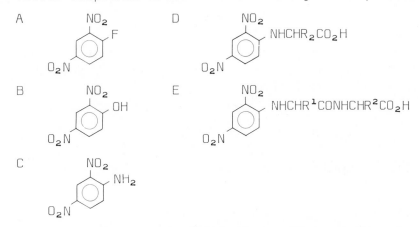

5. Which of the following would have the greatest effect on the R_f value of the dinitrophenyl amino acid?

A   The type of paper used in the chromatogram.

B   The temperature at which the chromatogram is run.

C   The type of solvent used to develop the chromatogram.

D   The quantity of substance used in the original spot.

E   The direction in which the solvent is run, e.g. upwards or downwards.

(Answers on page 92)

A further development in the separation and identification of amino acids is the use of ion-exchange resins in column chromatography, using high pressure to speed up the elution. This technique has been automated so that separations can be done very efficiently and rapidly. You may wish to read about ion-exchange chromatography in an up-to-date textbook.

Having completed a study of proteins, we now consider another important group of big molecules - the carbohydrates.

CARBOHYDRATES

The name 'carbohydrate' was first used to refer to any substance with an empirical formula $(C:H_2O)_n$. The title is misleading because carbohydrates are not hydrated in the usual sense of the word, i.e. they do not contain relatively loosely-attached water molecules.

The empirical formula arises from the fact that molecules of carbohydrates consist mainly of the repeating structural unit:

$$H-\overset{\textstyle |}{\underset{\textstyle |}{C}}-OH$$

The presence of many — OH groups influences the properties of carbohydrates, but there is also an important contribution from a $>C=O$ group or a — CHO group which is invariably present as well.

The simplest carbohydrates are known as sugars, and these are subdivided into monosaccharides, such as glucose, and disaccharides, such as sucrose. Natural polymers made up from simple sugar sub-units are known as poly- saccharides, e.g. starch and cellulose.

Sugars - an introduction

In this section we look at the way sugars are named, conventions for writing their structural formulae and the shapes of their molecules.

Objectives. When you have finished this section you should be able to:

(50)   explain the difference between an aldose and a ketose;

(51)   write simple structural formulae for the open-chain structures of glucose and fructose;

(52)   indicate the difference in structure between the D- and L-forms of glucose and fructose;

(53)   indicate the difference between the α- and β-isomers of D-glucose by drawing simplified structural formulae;

(54)   describe what takes place during the mutarotation of glucose.

Skim through the chapter of your textbook which deals with sugars. Locate the sections which deal with the topics mentioned above and return to them to help you answer the exercises which follow.

Exercise 45   In any sugar molecule, one
               carbon atom bears a carbonyl
               group and all the other carbon
               atoms bear hydroxy groups.
               One example is D-glucose,
               which is shown in its
               'chain' form in Fig. 22.

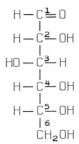

Fig. 22.   A glucose molecule

(a)   Is D-glucose an aldose or a ketose? Explain.

(b)   Which other classifying name, based on the number of carbon
      atoms, could be applied to glucose?

(c)   In D-glucose the carbonyl group is at C^1. In some sugars,
      the carbonyl group is at another position. Which position
      is this and what type of sugar has the carbonyl group there?

(d)   How is the structure of D-fructose related to that of D-
      glucose?

(e)   Explain why there are a great many stereo-isomers of D-
      glucose. How is the structure of L-glucose related to that
      of D-glucose? Why does L-glucose cost 300 times as much as
      D-glucose?

(Answers on page 93)

In addition to the 'chain' form, both D-glucose and D-fructose exist in two
'ring' forms, with names prefixed by the Greek letters α and β. The three-
dimensional structure of α-D-glucose is shown in Fig. 23 as a 'puckered ring'
with a more-easily-drawn shorthand version alongside. Notice that in the
shorthand version, the ring is drawn flat, and some of the carbon and
hydrogen atoms are omitted for simplicity.

Fig. 23.   Conventional and shorthand structures for α-D-glucose

We suggest that you make a model of α-D-glucose $(C_6H_{12}O_6)$ to see how
these two ways of drawing the structure relate to the three-
dimensional shape.

The next exercise concerns the interconversion of the chain and ring
forms of D-glucose.

Exercise 46   Fig. 24 shows the equilibria which exist in an aqueous
              solution of D-glucose.

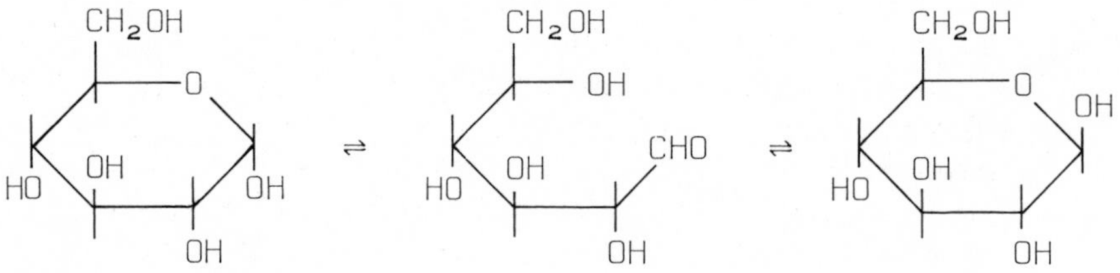

Fig. 24.   Mutarotation of glucose

(a)   On a copy of Fig. 24:

      (i)   label the α- and β- forms of D-glucose,

      (ii) number the carbon atoms to correspond with Fig. 22
            on page 56.

(b)   Describe briefly the difference in the structures of the
      α- and β- forms. Are these two forms enantiomers?

(c)   Some pure α-D-glucose is dissolved in water and its optical
      rotation is observed in a polarimeter. What happens and
      what is this change called?

(d)   Approximately what percentage of D-glucose exists in
      solution as the open-chain form?

(e)   Why are the two ring forms sometimes called α- and β-
      glucopyranose? (Hint: look up the structure of the
      compound called pyran.)

(Answers on page 93)

The next exercise is about D-fructose, which also exists in α- and β- forms,
but in this case the rings have five members rather than 6.

Exercise 47   (a)   Draw the straight-chain structure of D-fructose
                    (see Exercise 45(d) and Fig. 22 on page 53).

              (b)   Why does D-fructose form a 5-membered ring rather than a
                    6-membered ring?

              (c)   By analogy with Fig. 24, sketch the structure of
                    α-D-fructose.

              (d)   Would you expect α-D-fructose to undergo mutarotation?

              (e)   Why is α-D-fructose sometimes called α-D-fructofuranose?
                    (Hint: look up the structure of the compound called furan.)

              (Answers on page 93)

In the next section we explain the use of the D- and L- notation. Your
teacher may tell you to omit it.

Configuration of sugars

All sugars are related to glyceraldehyde (a triose) and can, in theory at least, be synthesized from it. Glyceraldehyde has a single chiral centre and there are, therefore, two optically-active forms (enantiomers). The prefixes D- and L- applied to the names of sugars indicate how the sugars are related to the two enantiomers of glyceraldehyde shown below.

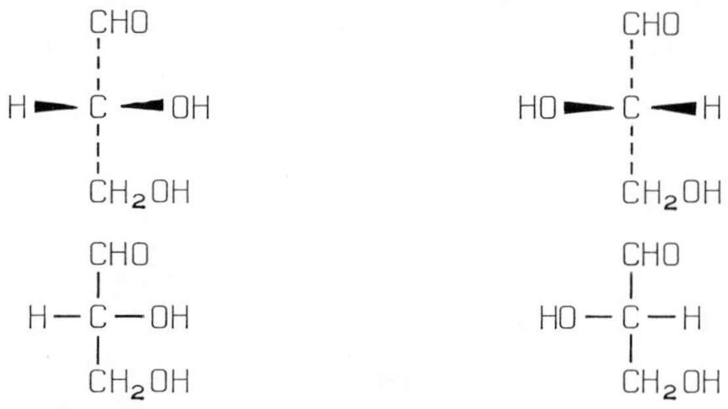

```
        CHO                           CHO
         |                             |
   H ►── C ──◄ OH             HO ►── C ──◄ H
         |                             |
        CH₂OH                         CH₂OH

        CHO                           CHO
         |                             |
   H ── C ── OH               HO ── C ── H
         |                             |
        CH₂OH                         CH₂OH

   D-glyceraldehyde              L-glyceraldehyde
```

In the 'flat' or 'projection' formulae it is assumed that the two atoms attached to the right and left of the central carbon atom are above the plane of the paper (the bond is sometimes shown as ◄──) while the other two atoms are below the plane of the paper (the bond is sometimes shown as -------).

Other sugars have a similar structure to glyceraldehyde in that a chain of varying length (Y in the diagram below) is substituted for the — CHO group. The nature of Y determines the name of the sugar; the relative positions of the — H and — OH groups on the final asymmetric carbon atom determines whether it is the D- or L- form.

```
         Y                             Y
         |                             |
   H ── C ── OH               HO ── C ── H
         |                             |
        CH₂OH                         CH₂OH
      D-sugar                       L-sugar
```

It so happens that D-glyceraldehyde and D-glucose are dextrorotatory but there is no obvious link between absolute configuration and optical rotation - some D-sugars are laevorotatory.

All naturally-occurring sugars are in the D-form because they are synthesized by stereospecific enzymes. (For similar reasons, all naturally-occurring amino acids are in the L-form.) Writers sometimes speculate about extra-terrestrial life-forms which could be built up from L-sugars and D-amino acids!

The sugars we have discussed so far are all monosaccharides. We now look briefly at disaccharides.

Disaccharides

Disaccharides have molecules consisting of two simple sugar units (such as glucose and fructose) linked together.

Objective. When you have finished this section you should be able to:

(55) state the sub-units from which molecules of <u>sucrose and maltose</u> are constructed;

(56) write the structural formula for sucrose.

Read about <u>disaccharides,</u> particularly maltose and sucrose. Look for the nature of the link between the two monosaccharide sub-units. Then you should be able to do the next exercise.

Exercise 48 (a) Which monomers are joined together to form

   (i) maltose,

   (ii) sucrose?

   (b) By what type of reaction might sucrose and maltose be formed from sugar units?

   (c) Draw the structural formula of sucrose.

   (Answers on page 93)

In the next section we look at polysaccharides, the polymers constructed from many sugar units linked together in the same way as they are in disaccharides.

Polysaccharides

Polysaccharides are often classified according to their function as <u>structural</u> and <u>storage</u> materials. In this section we consider an important structural polysaccharide (cellulose) and two storage polysaccharides (starch and glycogen). All three are homopolymers of glucose.

As you will find if you go on to study any biochemistry, there are more complex polysaccharides, copolymers with two different repeating units, such as the ones found in bacterial cell walls. However, you do not need to know these for A-level chemistry.

Objectives. When you have finished this section you should be able to:

(57) explain the difference between α- and β-glycosidic linkages;

(58) indicate how the structures of <u>amylose</u>, <u>amylopectin</u>, <u>cellulose</u> and <u>glycogen</u> differ;

(59) state examples of the main storage and structural polysaccharides in plant and animal cells.

Read the section on polysaccharides in your textbook(s). Find out
how the glucose units are joined together in cellulose, starch and
glycogen, noting the two types of chains found in starch as amylose
and amylopectin. Also, look for an explanation of how enzymes break
these three substances down and when you would get a limit dextrin.
Make brief notes on the structure and function of each polysaccharide
and then attempt the exercise which follows.

Exercise 49 (a) Glycogen is found in animal cells while plants
                  contain amylose, amylopectin and cellulose.
                  Explain briefly the functions of the three under-
                  lined polysaccharides.

            (b) Give a structural difference between the following pairs of
                 polysaccharides:

                   (i)   amylose and amylopectin,

                  (ii)   amylopectin and glycogen,

                 (iii)   glycogen and cellulose.

            (Answers on page **94**)

In the next section you study the reactions of sugars and polysaccharides.
We have collected all the practical work together into a single experiment.
Your teacher will advise you which parts are important for your
syllabus.

The reactions of carbohydrates

Many of the reactions shown by sugars will already be familiar to you from
your previous studies of the carbonyl and hydroxyl groups.

Objectives. When you have finished this section you should be able to:

(60) write equations for the reaction of glucose with Fehling's solution,
      Tollens' reagent, phenylhydrazine and 2,4-dinitrophenylhydrazine;

(61) explain what happens during the acid hydrolysis of sucrose and
      starch;

(62) explain the principle by which a polarimeter works;

(63) explain the difference between a reducing and a non-reducing sugar
      and carry out a test for each type.

Experiment 4 now follows. Work through the part(s) needed for your
syllabus.

EXPERIMENT 4
Reactions of carbohydrates

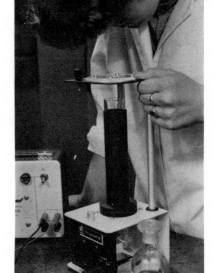

Aim

The purpose of this experiment is to illustrate the reactions of some sugars and the
polysaccharide starch.

Introduction

This experiment is divided into five parts;

A. Dehydration. Here you examine the effect of heat and of concentrated
    sulphuric acid on sugars.

B. Oxidation. You use Fehling's and Tollens' reagents to test sugars for
    reducing power.

C. Carbonyl derivatives. You make the 2,4-dinitrophenylhydrazone and the
    phenylhydrazone of a sugar.

D. Hydrolysis. You examine the effects of hot dilute acid and saliva on
    sucrose and starch.

E. Polarimetry. You use a polarimeter to observe the rotation of plane-
    polarized light by sugars and to follow the hydrolysis of sucrose.

General requirements for Parts A, B, C and D

safety spectacles
6 test-tubes in a rack
beaker, 250 cm^3 (for use as a water-bath)
Bunsen burner, tripod, gauze and bench mat
wash-bottle of distilled water
spatula
glucose, $C_6H_{12}O_6$
fructose, $C_6H_{12}O_6$
sucrose, $C_{12}H_{22}O_{11}$
maltose, $C_{12}H_{22}O_{11}$
starch, $(C_6H_{11}O_5)n$
sulphuric acid, dilute, 1 M H_2SO_4

Part A

protective gloves
sulphuric acid, concentrated, H_2SO_4
wood splint
limewater, $Ca(OH)_2(aq)$
potassium dichromate(VI) solution, 0.1 M $K_2Cr_2O_7$
filter paper strips

Part B

Fehling's solutions 1 and 2
ammonia solution, 2 M NH_3
silver nitrate solution, 0.05 M $AgNO_3$

Part C

2,4-dinitrophenylhydrazine solution
phenylhydrazinium chloride, $C_6H_5NHNH_3Cl$
sodium ethanoate, hydrated, $CH_3CO_2Na\cdot3H_2O$

Part D

boiling water-bath
ammonia solution, 2 M NH_3
litmus paper
Fehling's solution or Tollens' reagent as in part B
iodine solution, 0.1 M I_2 in KI(aq)

Part E

simple polarimeter

Hazard warning

Concentrated sulphuric acid is very corrosive and reacts violently
with water, especially when hot. Therefore you MUST:

WEAR SAFETY SPECTACLES AND PROTECTIVE GLOVES,
USE SMALL QUANTITIES AND COOL RESIDUES BEFORE DISPOSAL,
POUR COLD RESIDUES SLOWLY INTO PLENTY OF COLD WATER, STIRRING TO DISPERSE HEAT

Fehling's solution 2 is corrosive because it contains sodium hydroxide
It is likely to spurt out of a test-tube during heating.
Therefore you MUST:

WEAR SAFETY SPECTACLES
ENSURE THAT NOBODY IS IN LINE WITH A TEST-TUBE DURING HEATING.

Tollens' reagent can become explosive if allowed to evaporate to
dryness. Therefore you MUST:

WASH AWAY RESIDUES WITH PLENTY OF WATER

Procedure

A. Dehydration

1. Warm about 0.5 g of glucose or sucrose in a dry test-tube. Use a low
   flame and heat the tube gently. Record your observations in a copy of
   Results Table 4, noting particularly any changes in state, colour,
   viscosity and smell.

2. Carefully add about 1 cm³ of concentrated sulphuric acid to about
   0.5 g of glucose or sucrose in a test-tube.

3. Warm the mixture gently and then remove the tube from the flame to
   observe and record the changes which occur without further heating.

4. Heat the mixture more strongly and test for carbon monoxide, carbon
   dioxide and sulphur dioxide.

B. Oxidation

1. Dissolve about 0.1 g of glucose in 2 cm³ distilled water in a test-tube.

2. Add 1 cm³ each of Fehling's solutions 1 and 2. Heat the tube
   carefully to keep the mixture <u>just</u> boiling for about 30 seconds.

3. Note the colour of the solution and whether any precipitate is formed.

4. Repeat steps 1 to 3 using fructose, maltose and sucrose.

5. Prepare some ammoniacal silver nitrate solution (Tollen's reagent) for your own use as follows. Add ammonia solution drop by drop to about 5 cm³ of silver nitrate solution until the resulting buff precipitate <u>almost</u> redissolves on shaking.

6. Dissolve about 0.1 g of glucose in 2 cm³ distilled water in a <u>clean</u> test-tube.

7. Add about 2 cm³ of Tollens' reagent and heat the tube in a beaker of boiling water. Note any colour change that takes place.

8. Repeat steps 5 to 7 with fructose, maltose and sucrose.

C. <u>Carbonyl derivatives</u>

1. Dissolve about 0.5 g of glucose in 1 cm³ distilled water and add 5 cm³ of 2,4-dinitrophenylhydrazine solution.

2. If crystals do not form, add a little dilute sulphuric acid, warm the test-tube and then cool under running cold water.

3. Weigh out 0.2 g of glucose or fructose, 0.4 g phenylhydrazinium chloride and 0.6 g hydrated sodium ethanoate and transfer into a clean, dry test-tube.

4. Add 4 cm³ distilled water.

5. Note the time and heat in a boiling water bath, shaking the tube occasionally.

6. Record the time when crystals first appear.

7. If you have time, ask for extra apparatus so that you can filter the crystals, wash with a little distilled water, dry between filter papers and recrystallize from ethanol.

8. Measure the melting-point of a dried sample of the purified crystals and compare it with the value given in tables of melting-points.

D. (a) <u>Hydrolysis of sucrose</u>

1. Take about 0.3 g sucrose, add 4 cm³ distilled water and shake to dissolve. Add 1 cm³ of dilute sulphuric acid.

2. Heat the tube in a boiling-water bath for 5 minutes.

3. Add enough dilute aqueous ammonia to neutralize the solution.

4. Carry out a test with either Fehling's solution or Tollens' reagent to see whether you can detect any reducing sugar.

D. (b) <u>Hydrolysis of starch</u>

1. Place about 2 cm³ of starch solution in each of four test-tubes labelled A, B and C and D.

2. Add a little saliva solution to each of tubes A and B.

3. Boil the contents of tube A for 2 or 3 minutes, then place both tubes A and B in a water-bath at 40 °C for 20 minutes.

4. Add 1 cm³ dilute sulphuric acid to C and place it in a boiling water-bath for 15 minutes.

5. Neutralize solution C with dilute aqueous ammonia.

6. Divide the contents of each of the four tubes into two parts. Add two or three drops of iodine solution to one part and test the other with Fehling's solution or Tollens' reagent as in part B of this experiment.

Results Table 4

Experiment	Observations				
	Glucose	Fructose	Sucrose	Maltose	Starch
A. Dehydration (a) Action of heat (b) Sulphuric acid					
B. Oxidation (a) Fehling's soln. (b) Tollen's reagent					
C. Carbonyl derivatives (a) 2,4-dinitro- phenylhydrazone (b) Phenylhydrazone					
D. Hydrolysis					

(Specimen results on page **94**)

E. Polarimetry

We assume that
you will use a
polarimeter
like this one
shown in
Fig. 25.
If this is not
the case, ask
your teacher
to modify our
instructions.

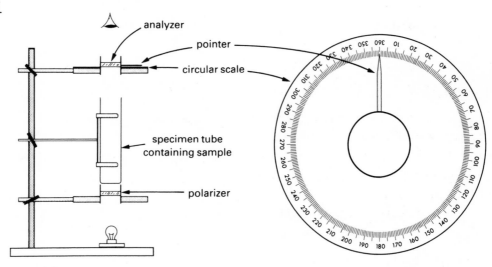

Fig. 25. A simple polarimeter

1. Remove the specimen tube and look vertically down at the light source
    through both polaroid films. If possible, insert a filter to limit the
    light to a narrow band of wavelengths.

2. Rotate the analyzer until you find a position which allows no light (or
    hardly any) to pass, and set the pointer to zero.

3. Fill the specimen tube with a fairly concentrated solution of glucose.

4. Place the specimen tube in position. Note, in a copy of Results Table 5,
    the new setting of the analyzer which extinguishes the light.

5. Halve the light-path in the liquid by pouring away half of the solution.
    Note the new setting of the analyzer which extinguishes the light.

6. Refill the specimen tube by adding distilled water. Again, adjust the
    analyzer and note the new setting.

If you have time, you may like to try another short experiment.

1. Dissolve 50 g of sucrose in 50 cm³ of hot water and leave to cool.

2. Add 20 cm³ of concentrated hydrochloric acid, mix well and pour into the polarimeter tube.

3. Take a reading, α_t, of the setting of the analyzer and note the time, t. Record your results in a copy of Results Table 5.

4. Take further readings at intervals as shown until there is no further change. 60 minutes should be enough for α_∞.

Results Table 5

Glucose	Movement of analyzer from zero			
	Initial	½ volume	Diluted	+ indicates clockwise
				− indicates anticlockwise
Sucrose	Time, t/min			0	3	6	10	15	20	30	∞
	Analyzer reading, α_t/°										
	$\alpha_t - \alpha_\infty$/°										

(Specimen results on page **94**)

Questions

A. 1. What are the main products when concentrated sulphuric acid reacts with glucose?

2. Why is this reaction called a dehydration?

3. What happens to the sulphuric acid during the reaction?

B. 4. Name the products formed when Tollens' reagent and Fehling's solution react with glucose.

5. Explain why glucose and fructose, but not sucrose, reduce silver(I) and copper(II) in solution.

C. 6. Give the common name and formula of the product formed when glucose or fructose reacts with phenylhydrazine. (The same product in each case.)

D. 7. Write an equation for the hydrolysis of sucrose.

8. Why is this reaction known as the <u>inversion</u> of sucrose?

9. Name the enzyme, found in yeast, which catalyses this reaction.

E. 10. Calculate the concentration of the solution of glucose which you used, given the following information.

The rotation caused by a 10 cm* column of solution at a concentration of 1 g cm⁻³* is constant for a given substance and is known as the specific rotation, [α]. [α] (D-glucose) = +52.5° cm³ g⁻¹ dm⁻¹

Specific rotation is related to observed rotation, α, by the expression:

$$[\alpha] = \frac{\alpha}{lc}$$

l (in dm*) is the length of the light path in the solution, and c is the concentration (g cm⁻³*)

*Note the unusual units.

(Strictly speaking, the wavelength of the polarized light and the temperature should also be constant at specified values, but you may ignore these for an approximate calculation.)

11. If you did the hydrolysis of sucrose experiment with the polarimeter, plot a graph of $(\alpha_t - \alpha_\infty)$ against t. Comment on its shape.

(Answers on page 95)

To help consolidate your knowledge of the reactions of sugars and polysaccharides, attempt the following Teacher-marked Exercise.

Teacher-marked Exercise   Distinguish between a mono-saccharide, a disaccharide and a polysaccharide, giving a specific example of each. Compare and contrast the reactions of glucose and of starch with:

(a) iodine,

(b) alkaline Cu^{2+}(aq) (Fehling's solution),

(c) dilute aqueous sulphuric acid,

(d) ammoniacal silver nitrate (Tollens' reagent).

We now consider, very briefly, another important group of biological polymers, nucleic acids.

NUCLEIC ACIDS

These remarkable substances, found both inside and outside the cell nucleus, are capable of reproducing themselves and of storing the information needed to assemble hundred of amino acids in the correct order for making protein molecules. In this section you examine the chemical composition of deoxyribonucleic acid (DNA) and ribonucleic acid (RNA) and see how their structures fit them for their biological function.

Objectives. When you have finished this section you should be able to:

(64) name the three components of a nucleotide;

(65) show how polynucleotides are formed from nucleotides;

(66) identify purine and pyrimidine bases from their formulae and show how one base of each type can be linked by hydrogen bonds;

Nucleic acids, like proteins, consist of long chains containing a great many sub-units. However, whereas a protein may have twenty different sub-units (amino acids), nucleic acids usually have only four, called nucleotides. Because of this, nucleic acids are often called polynucleotides.

Each nucleotide consists of three parts:

1. a monosaccharide (usually ribose or deoxyribose),
2. phosphoric(V) acid (esterified with an — OH group in the sugar),
3. a base (attached by condensation with another — OH group in the sugar).

In a polynucleotide, each phosphoric acid molecule becomes esterified with two sugar units, forming what is conveniently called the 'sugar-phosphate' backbone, to which four different bases are attached at regular intervals.

It is the order in which these four bases are attached that distinguishes the DNA molecules of different species and encodes all the genetic information necessary for cell replication and protein synthesis.

Read about nucleic acids in a textbook of organic chemistry or simple biochemistry. Look for the difference in the sugar/phosphate back-bone between DNA and RNA. Also notice which purine and pyrimidine bases are attached to the sugar/phosphate backbone and the way in which hydrogen bonding holds pairs of chains together. You need not attempt to learn the complete structures but should find enough information to be able to do the exercise which follows:

Exercise 50   Fig. 26 shows the sugar phosphate backbones of two DNA chains with attached purine and pyrimidine bases.

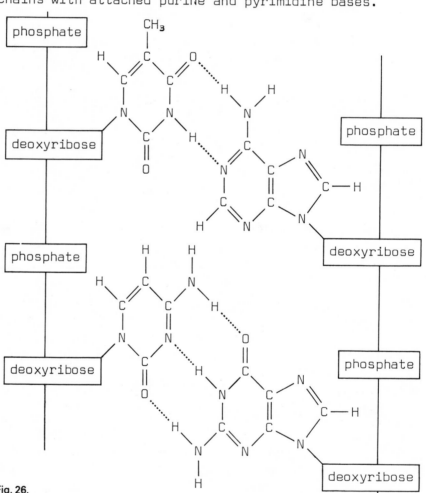

Fig. 26.

(a)   Name the purine bases and pyrimidine bases.

(b)   On a copy of Fig. 26 draw in the sites where you would expect hydrogen bonding to take place.

(c)   State two ways in which an RNA polynucleotide differs in structure from a DNA polynucleotide.

(Answers on page 95)

As you saw in the exercise you have just completed, the two strands of DNA are joined by their pairs of complementary bases. Normally, the chains are twisted into the famous double helix, shown as a diagram in Fig. 27 and as a model on the cover of this Unit.

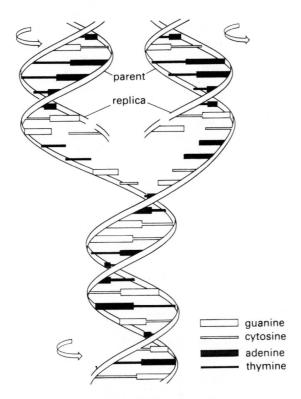

Fig. 27. Replication of the DNA double helix

However, if the chains separate from each other, as shown in Fig. 27, the base pairing enables a replica chain to build up from each parent chain. This is the basis of DNA replication which takes place during cell division or whenever a new protein is to be synthesized.

For protein synthesis, however, an RNA molecule builds up on part of the parent DNA strand and moves outside the nucleus to the ribosomes. Here, it acts as a template. Every group of three bases (a triplet) is the code for a particular amino acid so that the appropriate amino acids for a particular protein gradually assemble in the right order.

Each step of DNA replication and protein synthesis is catalyzed by a specific enzyme, another protein, which enables the reaction to take place at the temperature and under the conditions prevailing in the cell. Protein synthesis and DNA replication are fascinating topics which we cannot cover in detail in this course but which you would learn more about in a more advanced biochemistry or cell biology course.

For background information about the way in which scientists worked out the structure of DNA, you should read 'The Double Helix' by J.D. Watson. The book also gives a fascinating insight into the way scientific work is done and the rivalries (friendly and otherwise) between separate groups working on the same problem.

We now move on to a brief consideration of lipids. These are large molecules but not polymers. We include them for completeness as they are fundamental cell components.

LIPIDS

The term 'lipid' is applied to a wide range of substances which are insoluble in water but soluble in non-polar organic solvents. Most of these are esters which have large molecules and there are four main groups, the most familiar being glycerides (often known simply as 'fats'). In this section you extend the knowledge of glycerides you gained from Level One and look briefly at some other classes of lipid.

Objectives. When you have finished this section you should be able to:

(67) recognise the main groups of lipid and their biological functions;

(68) explain the physical differences between saturated and unsaturated fats in terms of the structure of their carboxylic acids.

There are four main groups of lipid.

1. Glycerides (fats). These are esters of glycerol (1,2,3-propanetriol) and long-chain carboxylic acids ('fatty acids'). Glycerides form the main energy storage material in plant and animal cells.

2. Waxes. These are mostly esters of long-chain monohydric alcohols and fatty acids. Waxes form protective coatings on skin, fur, feathers, leaves and fruits.

3. Compound lipids such as phospholipids. These can be regarded as glycerides with one of the ester groups replaced by another group, usually a nitrogenous base attached via a phosphate link. Phospholipids are important structural components of cell membranes.

4. Steroids. These are derived from the saturated hydrocarbon represented by the formula shown to the right. They include the male and female sex hormones, the digestive bile acids and 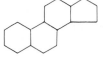 cholesterol. An excess of chlesterol has been linked with 'hardening of arteries' (arteriosclerosis) and heart disease.

Revise the work you did on fats in Level One and, if necessary, read an account of triglycerides so that you can do the following exercises.

Exercise 51   Refer to Table 8 on page 67 for this exercise.

Given that the double bonds in naturally-occurring fatty acids are normally in the *cis* configuration, state and explain:

(a) the trends in melting-point which occur in both saturated and unsaturated fatty acids,

(b) the difference in melting-point between saturated and unsaturated fatty acids with the same number of carbon atoms per molecule.

(Answers on page **95**)

Table 8   The melting-points of some naturally-occurring fatty acids

C	Formula	Systematic name	Common name	M-Pt. /°C
12	$CH_3(CH_2)_{10}COOH$	Dodecanoic acid	Lauric acid	44.2
14	$CH_3(CH_2)_{12}COOH$	Tetradecanoic	Myristic	53.9
16	$CH_3(CH_2)_{14}COOH$	Hexadecanoic	Palmitic	63.1
18	$CH_3(CH_2)_{16}COOH$	Octadecanoic	Stearic	69.6
20	$CH_3(CH_2)_{18}COOH$	Eicosanoic	Arachidic	76.5
24	$CH_3(CH_2)_{22}COOH$	Tetracosanoic	Lignoceric	86.0
16	$CH_3(CH_2)_5CH{=}CH(CH_2)_7COOH$		Palmitoleic	-0.5
18	$CH_3(CH_2)_7CH{=}CH(CH_2)_7COOH$		Oleic	13.4
18	$CH_3(CH_2)_4CH{=}CHCH_2CH{=}CH(CH_2)_7COOH$		Linoleic	-5
18	$CH_3CH_2CH{=}CHCH_2CH{=}CHCH_2CH{=}CH(CH_2)_7COOH$		Linolenic	-11
20	$CH_3(CH_2)_4CH{=}CHCH_2CH{=}CHCH_2CH{=}CHCH_2CH{=}CH(CH_2)_3COOH$		Arachidonic	-49.5

Exercise 52   There is strong evidence to show that a high proportion of saturated fatty acids in a person's diet contributes to heart disease. Use the information in Table 9, below, to recommend a fat or oil which someone with a tendency to heart disease should:

(a) avoid eating in large quantities,

(b) use in their diet where possible.

Give a brief explanation for your choices.

(Answers on page 96)

Table 9   Fatty acid composition of fats and oils

| | Saturated acids (%) | | | | | | | Unsaturated acids (%) | | | | Other |
| | | | | | | | | Enoic (i.e. one double bond) | | | | |
Fat or oil	C_8	C_{10}	C_{12}	C_{14}	C_{16}	C_{18}	$>C_{18}$	$<C_{16}$	C_{16}	C_{18}	$>C_{18}$	C_{18}
Beef tallow			0.2	2-3	25-30	21-26	0.4-1	0.5	2-3	39-42	0.3	2
Butter	1-2	2-3	1-4	8-13	25-32	8-13	0.4-2	1-2	2-5	22-29	0.2-1.5	3
Coconut	5-9	4-10	44-51	13-18	7-10	1-4				5-8	0-1	1-3
Corn				0-2	8-10	1-4			1-2	30-50	0-2	34-56
Cottonseed				0-3	17-23	1-3				23-44	0-1	34-55
Lard				1	25-30	12-16		0.2	2-5	41-51	2-3	3-8
Olive			0-1	0-2	7-20	1-3	0-1		1-3	53-86	0-3	4-22
Palm				1-6	32-47	1-6				40-52		2-11
Palm kernel	2-4	3-7	45-52	14-19	6-9	1-3	1-2		0-1	10-18		1-2
Peanut				0.5	6-11	3-6	5-10		1-2	39-66		17-38
Soybean				0.3	7-11	2-5	1-3		0-1	22-34		50-70

LEVEL TWO CHECKLIST

You have now reached the end of this Unit. Look again at the checklist at
the end of Level One. In addition, assuming you have done the whole Unit,
you should now be able to:

(21) & (22)   write the <u>general formula of α-amino acids</u> and state some
                   <u>systematic names</u>;

(23)   recognise an <u>optically-active amino acid</u> from its formula;

(24)   explain how the <u>physical properties of amino acids</u> provide evidence
       for the existence of <u>zwitterions</u>;

(25) & (26)   write equations for the <u>reactions of an amino acid</u> with acids
                   and alkalis and distinguish between <u>acidic, basic and neutral</u>
                   amino acids;

(27)   explain the term <u>isoelectric point</u> and show how amino acid solutions
       act as <u>buffers</u>;

(28) & (29)   describe the reactions of an amino acid with <u>nitrous acid,</u>
                 <u>ethanol, ethanoic anhydride, soda-lime and copper(II) ions</u>;

(30)   outline two general methods for the <u>preparation of amino acids</u>;

(31) & (32)   write a generalised equation for the formation of a <u>peptide</u>
                 <u>link</u> and explain why amino acids do not readily form such
                 links in ordinary conditions;

(33)   explain the terms <u>dipeptide</u>, <u>tripeptide</u> and <u>polypeptide</u>;

(34)   distinguish between a <u>fibrous</u> and a <u>globular</u> protein;

(35)   explain how <u>restricted rotation</u> around the peptide bond gives it a
       planar shape;

(36)   distinguish between the <u>primary</u>, <u>secondary</u> and <u>tertiary</u> structures
       of a protein;

(37)   state and explain the roles of the <u>peptide bond</u>, <u>hydrogen bonding</u>,
       and <u>disulphide bridges</u> in protein structure;

(38)   explain what happens when a protein <u>denatures</u>;

(39)   state the reaction of <u>1-fluoro-2,4-dinitrobenzene (FDNB)</u> with an
       amino acid;

(40) & (42)   explain how <u>N-terminal analysis</u> of a polypeptide is carried out;

(41) & (43)   outline the role of <u>chromatography</u> and the use of <u>enzymes</u> such
                 as trypsin and carboxypeptidase in <u>sequence determination</u>;

(44)   explain the meanings of the terms <u>stationary and mobile phase</u>, <u>eluent</u>
       <u>and adsorbent</u>, <u>adsorption</u> and <u>partition</u>, in the context of chroma-
       tography;

(45)   outline the distinctive features of four types of chromatography,
       <u>column</u>, <u>thin-layer</u>, <u>paper</u>, and <u>gas-liquid</u>;

(46)   explain the difference between <u>ascending</u> and <u>descending</u> chromatography;

(47) to (49)   describe the <u>separation of amino acids</u> by paper chromatography,
               including the use of <u>ninhydrin</u> solution and the calculation of
               R_f values;

(50)   explain the difference between an <u>aldose</u> and <u>ketose</u>;

(51) & (52)   write simple structural formulae for the open-chain structures
              of glucose and fructose, indicating the difference between the
              D- and L- forms;

(53)   indicate the difference between the α- and β-isomers of D-glucose by
       drawing simplified structural formulae;

(54)   describe what takes place during the mutarotation of glucose;

(55) & (56)   state the sub-units from which molecules of sucrose and maltose
              are constructed and write the structural formula of sucrose;

(57)   explain the difference between α- and β-glycosidic linkages;

(58)   indicate how the structures of amylose, amylopectin, cellulose and
       glycogen differ;

(59)   name examples of the main storage and structural polysaccharides in
       plant and animal cells;

(60)   write equations for the reaction of glucose with Fehling's solution,
       Tollens' reagent, phenylhydrazine and 2,4-dinitrophenylhydrazine;

(61)   explain what happens during the acid hydrolysis of sucrose and starch;

(62)   explain the principle by which a polarimeter works;

(63)   explain the difference between a reducing and a non-reducing sugar
       and carry out a test for each type;

(64)   name the three components of a nucleotide;

(65)   show how polynucleotides are formed from nucleotides;

(66)   identify purine and pyrimidine bases from their formulae and show how
       one base of each type can be linked by hydrogen bonds;

(67)   recognise the main groups of lipid and their biological functions;

(68)   explain the physical differences between saturated and unsaturated fats
       in terms of the structure of their carboxylic acids.

END-OF-UNIT TEST

To find out how well you have learned the material in this Unit, try
the test which follows.   Read the notes below before starting:

1.   You should spend about 1½ hours on this test.

2.   Hand your answers to your teacher for marking.

END-OF-UNIT TEST

Questions 1-6 concern the following classes of organic compounds:

A   Ester   C   Nitrile   E   Salt

B   Amide   D   Acid anhydride

Select, from A to E, the heading under which you could best classify each of the following (where R_1, R_2, etc. are alkyl groups).

1.
   A protein,
$$\left[-N-\underset{\underset{H}{|}}{\underset{R_1}{|}}C-\underset{}{\overset{O}{\overset{||}{C}}}-N-\underset{\underset{H}{|}}{\underset{R_2}{|}}C-\underset{}{\overset{O}{\overset{||}{C}}}- \right]_n$$
(1)

2.   A fat,
$$\begin{array}{l} CH_2CO_2R_1 \\ | \\ CHCO_2R_2 \\ | \\ CH_2CO_2R_3 \end{array}$$
(1)

3.
$$CH_3CH_2-\overset{O}{\overset{||}{C}}-O-\overset{O}{\overset{||}{C}}-CH_2CH_3$$
(1)

4.
   Nylon,
$$\left[-N-(CH_2)_6-N-\overset{O}{\overset{||}{C}}-(CH_2)_4-\overset{O}{\overset{||}{C}}- \right]_n$$
(1)

5.   A soap, RCO_2Na

6.
   Terylene,
$$\left[-\overset{O}{\overset{||}{C}}-\underset{}{\bigcirc}-\overset{O}{\overset{||}{C}}-O-CH_2-O- \right]_n$$
(1)

Questions 7-10 refer to the classification of a substance as a

A   monosaccharide   D   polysaccharide-hydrolyzing enzyme

B   polysaccharide   E   protein-hydrolyzing enzyme

C   fat-hydrolyzing enzyme

Select, from A to E, the heading under which you would classify each of the following.

7.   Carboxypeptidase   (1)

8.   Lysozyme   (1)

9.   α-Amylase   (1)

10. Cellulose   (1)

11. A mixture of amino acids was subjected to two-way chromatography using butanol-ethanoic(acetic) acid and phenol successively as solvents. When the chromatogram was developed, spots were obtained as shown on the diagram below:

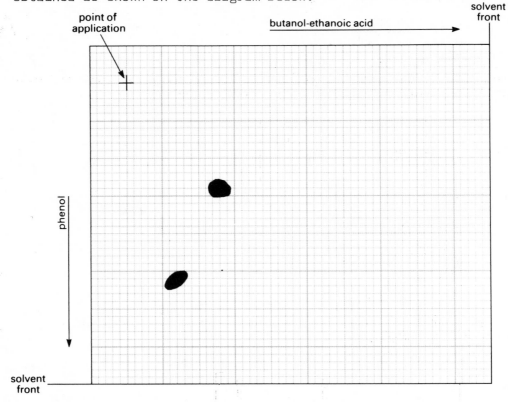

The R_f values for some amino acids are as follows:

Amino acid	R_f value in butanol-ethanoic acid	R_f value in phenol
Aspartic acid	0.24	0.14
Cystine	0.13	0.31
Glycine	0.26	0.35
Lysine	0.14	0.66
Serine	0.27	0.31
Valine	0.60	0.61

The correct composition of the amino acid mixture is

A   glycine and lysine   C   aspartic acid and cystine   E   serine and lysine

B   glycine and valine   D   serine and valine   (1)

12. Which of the following represents a dipeptide?

A $NH_3^+ - CH - CO_2^- NH_3^+ - CH - CO_2^-$
    $CH_2 - CO_2^- NH_3^+ (CH_2)_4$

B $NH_3^+ - CH - CO_2^-$
    $(CH_2)_2 CO_2^-$

C $NH_3^+ - CH - CO_2^-$ NH
    $(CH_2)_3 - NH - \overset{\parallel}{C} - NH_3^+$

D $NH_2 - CH - CO - NH - CH - CO_2^-$
    $(CH_2)_4 NH_3^+$ CH_3

E $NH_3^+ - CH - CO_2^-$ $NH_3^+ - CH - CO_2^-$
    $CH_2 - S - S - CH_2$

(1)

Questions 13 and 14 deal with the following laboratory situation.

A series of experiments was conducted in an attempt to elucidate the primary structure of a small polypeptide. The polypeptide was refluxed with 6 M hydrochloric acid and the hydrolysate subjected to two-way paper chromatography using a butan-1-ol ethanoic (acetic) acid mixture, and phenol solution, as solvents in turn. The R_f values for certain amino acids are:

		In butan-1-ol ethanoic acid mixture	In phenol solution
Alanine	(ala)	0.38	0.48
Aspartic acid	(asp)	0.24	0.14
Glutamic acid	(glu)	0.30	0.21
Glycine	(gly)	0.26	0.36
Lysine	(lys)	0.14	0.68
Phenylalanine	(phe)	0.68	0.70
Valine	(val)	0.60	0.63

The diagram shows some of the amino acids which appeared as purple spots on the chromatogram after spraying with ninhydrin and warming.

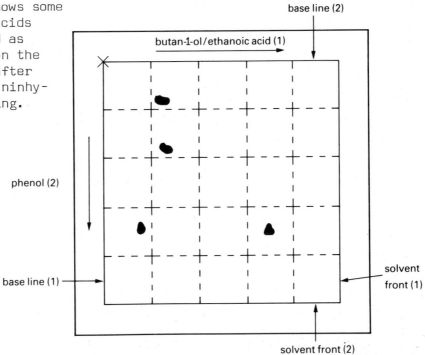

13. Why was two-way chromatography needed in this experiment?

    A Some amino acids are not soluble in the first solvent.

    B Some amino acids have nearly equal R_f values in one or other solvent.

    C Some amino acids have R_f values too high in the first solvent for it to be effective.

    D Some amino acids do not 'stain up' after separation using only the first solvent.

    E By using two solvents the separation is considerably speeded up. (1)

14. Which amino acids are shown by the chromatogram to be present in the polypeptide?

   A Asp, gly, lys, phe   D Asp, glu, lys, val

   B Asp, gly, lys, val   E Asp, glu, phe, val

   C Glu, gly, lys, val

   (1)

For questions 15 to 18 ONE or MORE of the responses given are correct. Answer as follows.

A if only 1, 2 and 3 are correct   D if only 4 is correct

B if only 1 and 3 are correct   E if some other response, or
                                        combination, is correct
C if only 2 and 4 are correct

15. Glucose and fructose

   1 are obtained from sucrose

   2 give a silver mirror with Tollen's reagent

   3 have the same molecular formula

   4 have four asymmetric carbon atoms

16. On hydrolysis, a polypeptide was found to yield the following dipeptides:

   Alanylleucine (A-L)   Leucylglycine (L-G)   Leucylleucine (L-L)

   Glycylleucine (G-L)   Leucylalanine (L-A)

   Possible sequences of amino acids in the polypeptide include

   1 L—L—G—L—A—L—G   3 L—A—L—L—G—L—A

   2 L—G—A—L—L—L—G   4 L—A—G—L—L—L—A

   (1)

17. The peptide of structure

$$H_2N-CH-CO-NH-CH-CO-NH-CH_2-CO-NH-CH-CO_2H$$
$$\qquad\quad |\qquad\qquad\qquad |\qquad\qquad\qquad\qquad\qquad\quad |$$
$$\qquad\quad CH_3\qquad\qquad\quad CH_2CO_2H\qquad\qquad\qquad (CH_2)_4NH_2$$

was subjected to N-terminal analysis using 1-fluoro-2,4-dinitrobenzene followed by acid hydrolysis. Which of the following would be included in the product?

(1)

18. Which of the following reagents would result in a reaction occurring with BOTH the —NH$_2$ and the —CO$_2$H group in glycine, H$_2$NCH$_2$CO$_2$H?

    A

    1 Ethanol and dry hydrogen chloride   3 Moist copper(II) carbonate

    2 Nitrous acid   4 Benzoyl chloride (C$_6$H$_5$COCl)

    (1)

For questions 19 and 20 choose an answer from A to E as follows:

A Both statements true: second explains first

B Both statements true: second does not explain first

C First true: second false

D First false: second true

E Both false

FIRST STATEMENT   SECOND STATEMENT

19. Sugar is very soluble in   The forces of attraction between
    cyclohexane.   cyclohexane molecules are stronger   A
                                      than those between sugar mole-
                                      cules.
                                                              (1)

20. Alanine, H$_2$NCH(CH$_3$)CO$_2$H, Alanine has a carbon atom with
    exists in optically   four different groups attached   A
    active forms.   to it.
                                                              (1)

21. (a) Describe briefly the preparation of aminoethanoic acid,
        starting from ethanoic acid.   (6)   A part

    (b) Write equations for two typical reactions of aminoethanoic
        acid.   (4)

    (c) Name and give one example of the natural polymers which are
        made from substances such as aminoethanoic acid. What is
        the name and structure of the characteristic functional
        group in such polymers.   (5)

    (d) Which of the two formulae below best represents aminoethanoic
        acid? Give the reason for your choice.   (3)

                H$_2$NCH$_2$COOH   H$_3$N$^+$CH$_2$COO$^-$

22. (a) Distinguish between an aldose and a ketose by drawing   A
        structural formulae for a named example of each, and show
        how each may be represented by both open chain and ring
        structures.   (8)

    (b) Explain why such compounds may be optically active. Suggest
        why the optical activity of a solution of dextro-rotatory
        sucrose alters during hydrolysis to monosaccharides. (6)

    (c) How might starch be converted into monosaccharides?
        Illustrate this change by a block diagram or an equation.
        Describe and explain TWO instances of difference in chemical
        behaviour between starch and its constituent monosaccharides. (6)

23. (a) Write the structural formula of the compound formed on treating glucose with hydroxylamine. (Configuration not required.) (2)

    (b) Write the structural formula of <u>one</u> organic compound, other than ethanoic acid, that could be formed when fructose is treated with ethanoic anhydride. (Configuration not required.) (2)

    (c) Describe briefly how glucose may be converted to a mono-hydric primary alcohol. (6)

24. Explain, giving <u>one</u> example in <u>each</u> case, the meaning of <u>each</u> of the following terms:

    condensation, polymerization, addition polymerization, cross-linking, a thermosetting plastic, a thermoplastic resin.

    (12)

    Describe the laboratory preparation of an addition polymer and discuss the mechanism of its formation. (6)

25. Give examples of the various types of compounds which are used as ionic detergents. Describe the action of detergents in the removal of oils or fats. (6)
    (8)

(Total 100 marks)

APPENDIX ONE

X-RAY CRYSTALLOGRAPHY

In Unit S4 (Bonding & Structure) we mentioned X-ray diffraction as a powerful technique for determining the arrangement of atoms and ions in crystals of simple substances. In this Unit, you learned that the technique reveals crystalline character in some polymers and has been used to work out very complex structures such as those of DNA and a number of proteins. So far you have focussed on the results of X-ray crystallography; now you consider the technique itself and the theory behind it.

Objectives. When you have finished this section you should be able to:

(69)   state the general conditions in which diffraction occurs giving rise to diffraction patterns, and give some specific examples;

(70)   describe, in non-mathematical terms, how X-ray diffraction patterns arise;

(71)   derive and use the Bragg equation;

(72)   outline one method of producing X-ray diffraction patterns;

(73)   describe briefly how X-ray diffraction helps to determine structures.

Diffraction patterns

All types of wave motion, including X-rays, interact with regularly-spaced arrays of particles, provided that the wavelength is about the same size as the spacing in the arrays. (The wavelength can be up to about 1000 times smaller than the spacing distance, but cannot be larger.) This interaction is known as diffraction, and the result of the interaction can be observed in the form of a diffraction pattern.

If you have studied physics you have probably seen some examples of diffraction patterns. If not, ask your teacher to demonstrate or to show you a film-loop.

The next exercise is about diffraction of different types of wave motion.

Exercise 53   For each wave motion in the list below, find out the approximate wavelength and choose the array of parti- cles most likely to give a diffraction pattern.

Wave motion	Array
Microwaves	Crystal
Water waves on a pond	Crystal model made from 5 cm spheres
Light (visible)	Row of fence posts or railings
X-rays	Piece of closely-woven cloth

(Answers on page 96)

Some examples of X-ray diffraction patterns, recorded on photographic film, are shown in Fig. 28. Each pattern is formed by the interaction of a beam of X-rays with a crystal or crystals, but the method used is slightly different in each case. You will read more about these methods later; first we consider how X-rays interact with crystals.

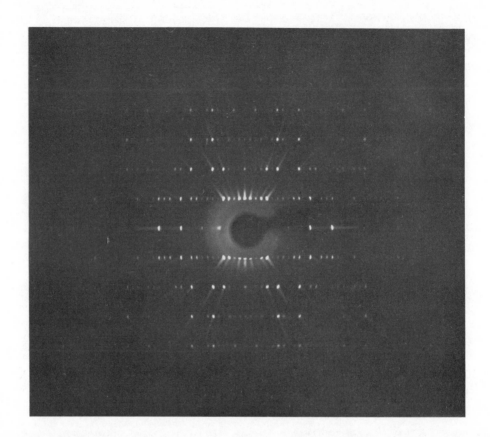

Fig.28. Some examples of X-ray diffraction patterns

You may also see X-ray diffraction patterns consisting of a series of concentric rings. The lower photograph in Fig. 28 is, in fact, a section of a circular pattern. Later in the Unit, you will read more about the different methods of obtaining X-ray diffraction patterns; first we consider how X-rays interact with crystals.

X-rays as wave motion

X-rays are a form of wave motion. In any wave motion, a disturbance of some
sort travels in the direction of the wave in such a wave that the size of the
disturbance varies like a sine curve. Fig. 29 shows how the disturbance at
any given <u>moment</u> varies with distance from the source of the wave. Fig. 30
shows how the disturbance at any given <u>point</u> in the path of the wave varies
with time.

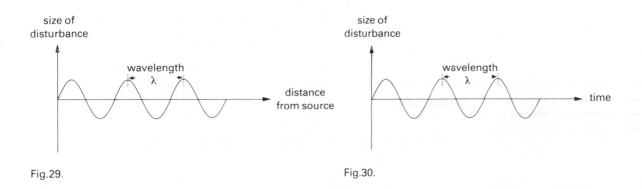

Fig.29.

Fig.30.

When ripples travel across a pond, the disturbance is a <u>vertical</u> movement of
water which causes a floating object to bob up and down as the waves pass it.
In X-rays the disturbance is an electric field at right angles to the
direction of the wave, as it is in all forms of electromagnetic waves including light, infra-red, ultra-violet, radio, radar, etc. These forms of
electromagnetic waves differ only in their wavelengths. X-rays have very
short wavelengths; radio-waves have long wavelengths.

Reinforcement and cancellation of waves

The principle behind the formation of all diffraction patterns is that each
particle in the grid or array scatters some of the radiation giving a whole
series of new waves travelling in all directions. Most of these new waves
cancel each other out but, in certain directions, they reinforce each other,
as shown in Fig. 31. The reinforced waves give rise to the spots on
diffraction patterns.

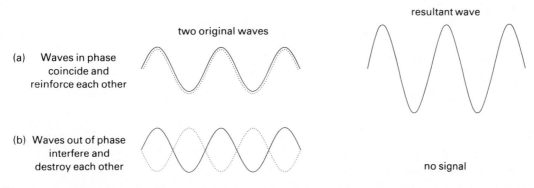

Fig. 31.

In the next section you learn how measurement of the angles between incident
wave and reinforced diffracted waves can give information about crystal
structure.

The Bragg Equation

W.H. and W.L. Bragg, father and son, simplified the mathematical treatment of the diffraction of X-rays, by considering it as <u>reflection</u> from <u>equally-spaced planes of atoms</u> in the crystal. Some examples of such planes are shown in two dimensions in Fig. 32 for a simple cubic lattice. Fig. 33 shows, in three dimensions, the more important planes in the three types of cubic lattice.

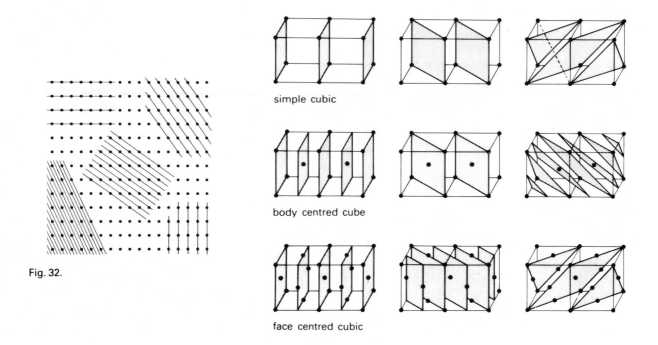

Fig. 32.

simple cubic

body centred cube

face centred cubic

Fig. 33. Planes of atoms in cubic lattices

The Braggs worked out an equation, known as the Bragg equation or Braggs' Law, which enabled them to calculate the spacings between the reflecting planes from measurements of the angles between reflected (or diffracted) beams and the undeflected beam.

You should study the derivation of the Bragg equation in your text-books so that you can do Exercise 54. However, as you read, you should bear in mind some points that are not always made clear:

1. You should regard the incident beam of X-rays as a <u>single</u> wave motion which is split (or reflected) by successive <u>layers</u> of atoms into a <u>number</u> of reflected beams which may or may not reinforce each other.

2. Most of the incident beam passes straight through the crystal undeflected. The reflected beams forming the diffraction pattern are relatively weak.

3. n in the Bragg equation is usually assumed to have a value of 1, but reflected beams also arise for $n = 2, 3$, etc., becoming weaker as n becomes larger.

Exercise 54   Fig. 34 shows the diffraction of X-rays by layers of
atoms in a crystal. The incident beam which is, of
course, very wide compared with the distance between
layers of atoms, can be represented by any straight line
in the direction of the beam. Two such lines, known as rays,
are shown. Each layer of atoms gives a weak reflected wave,
each represented by a single ray. In the example shown, the
reflected waves reinforce each other, giving a reflected beam of
X-rays which can be detected.

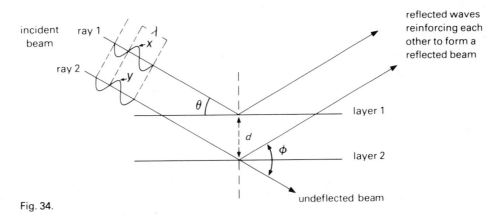

Fig. 34.

(a)   Although the path length of the two rays is diffe-
       rent, the diffracted rays are still in phase. On
       the diffracted rays draw the waves showing how the
       relative positions of the peaks x and y have changed.

(b)   During the X-ray diffraction of a sodium chloride
       crystal, a value of θ is obtained when the diffracted rays
       are still in phase, that is, they reinforce each other.
       What condition must be fulfilled for this to happen? Show
       any geometrical construction lines on the diagram.

(c)   Since the reflecting layers may not be
       parallel to the crystal surface, it is not   Not part
       possible to measure θ directly. The angle   of A-level
       ϕ, however, is easily measured. How is ϕ question
       related to θ?

(d)   Sir Lawrence Bragg, who carried out the first X-ray inves-
       tigation of sodium chloride, found that there were several
       values of θ, each giving rise to a peak on the detector
       trace, for which there was reinforcement of the diffracted
       rays. Also, he found that three different detector traces
       could be obtained according to the position of the crystal.

       Why are there several peaks on each trace in Fig. 35?

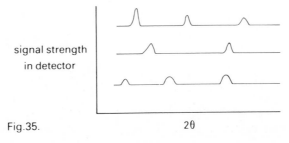

signal strength
in detector

Fig.35. 2θ

(e) Why is it possible to obtain three different traces?

(Answers on page 96)

81

Now that you have worked through the derivation of the Bragg equation, you should be able to do some calculations based on it.

Exercise 55   What is the distance between successive planes which reflect fairly strongly X-rays of wavelength 0.0583 nm at an angle of 9° to the planes?

(Answer on page **96**)

Exercise 56   The angle between the undeflected beam and a reflected beam of X-rays (wavelength 0.0635 nm) was found to be 47° 30'. Calculate three possible spacings between the reflecting planes. How, in practice, might you be able to tell which of the three is the one you want?

(Answer on page **96**)

Exercise 57   The Bragg equation can be used to determine the wavelength of X-rays, using a crystal of known dimensions. If the incident angle is 12° to a set of reflecting planes 0.198 nm apart, what is the wavelength of the X-rays? (Assume n = 1.)

(Answer on page **96**)

Methods for obtaining X-ray diffraction patterns

Find out from your textbook(s) how X-ray diffraction instruments are used. For examination purposes you need only know an outline of one method but, as most books describe several, we summarise the points of difference so that you can choose sensibly.

1. Nowadays the X-ray beam is always monochromatic (i.e. single wavelength). Early methods used a range of wavelengths which gave very complex patterns, difficult to interpret.

2. The X-ray beam may be directed at a single crystal or a powder consisting of many micro-crystals. A powder gives simple patterns consisting of rings rather than spots.

3. The diffracted beams may be detected by photographic film (flat or curved round the crystal) or by a Geiger-Muller tube which mechanically scans the space round the crystal. The G-M tube has the advantage of measuring the intensities of the beams as well as the angles.

If it is available, watch the section of the ILPAC video-programme 'Instrumental Techniques' which shows one particular instrument in use for X-ray crystallography. (Also shown is an unrelated technique called nuclear magnetic resonance. This is not likely to be on your syllabus, but may be of interest here because it complements X-ray diffraction. NMR is particularly useful in determining the positions of hydrogen atoms, which are not shown clearly by X-ray diffraction.)

Exercise 58 (a) In X-ray diffraction, why is the crystal rotated?

(b) Why do the spots in an X-ray diffraction pattern vary in intensity?

(c) Why do hydrogen atoms make very little oontribution to X-ray diffraction patterns?

(Answers on page 97)

Now that you have looked at some diffraction patterns and the methods by which they can be obtained, we consider briefly how they are interpreted.

Detailed analysis of X-ray diffraction patterns

Only general indications of the type of lattice can be obtained by simple inspection of diffraction patterns. However, it is possible, by use of a computerised mathematical technique called Fourier synthesis, to obtain detailed information about the electron distribution in the reflecting planes.

Another form of presentation, which is even more useful, is an electron contour map or electron-density map. You have interpreted such maps in Unit S4 (Bonding & Studcture) to identify ionic bonding and to obtain values of ionic radius. In the final exercise you interpret another electron-density map.

Exercise 59 The electron-density map below refers to a substance with the molecular formula $C_8H_8O_3$.

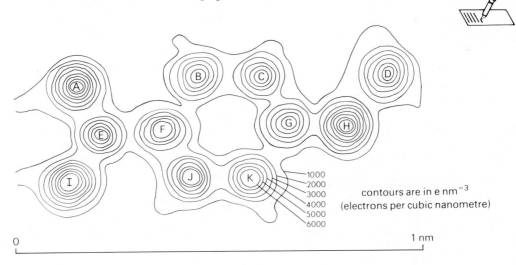

contours are in e nm^{-3}
(electrons per cubic nanometre)

Fig.36.

(a) What type of bonding is present? Explain.

(b) Identify the atoms lettered A-K.

(c) What information does the map give about the positions of hydrogen atoms?

(Answers on page 97)

ANSWERS

Exercise 1

Table 1 Ethene-based polymers

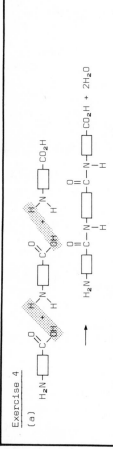

Group Y in monomer $CH_2=CHY$	Structural Formula of trimer ($n = 3$)	Repeating unit	Name(s) of polymer
—H			polyethene (polythene) (polyethylene)
—CH_3			polypropene (polypropylene)
—Cl			polychloroethene (polyvinylchloride) (PVC)
—CN			polypropenenitrile (polyacrylonitrile) (Acrilan)
(phenyl)			polyphenylethene (polystyrene)
—O—C(=O)—CH_3			polyethenylethanoate (polyvinylacetate) (PVA)

Exercise 2

Structure A.

Exercise 3

(a) A is isotactic (regular arrangement); B is atactic (irregular arrangement).

(b) Polyphenylethene (polystyrene) is usually atactic. Polypropene is usually isotactic.

Exercise 4

(a)

$$H_2N—\boxed{}—C(=O)—N(H)—\boxed{}—N(H)—C(=O)—\boxed{}—N(H)—CO_2H$$

(b) The —CONH— link is known as the peptide link (or bond). It may also be referred to as an amide link (or bond).

Exercise 5

(a) $HO_2C—\boxed{}—CO_2H + H_2N—\boxed{}—NH_2 \rightarrow HO_2C—\boxed{}—CONH—\boxed{}—NH_2 + H_2O$

(b)

(c) A homopolymer, such as the one in Exercise 3, is made from a single monomer. A copolymer, such as the one in this exercise, is made from two different monomers which alternate in the final structure.

Note that a copolymer has a single repeating unit in its structure (see (b) above) but this unit is itself made from two monomers.

Exercise 6

(a) $—(CH_2)_5CONH—$ or $—C(=O)—(CH_2)_5—N(H)—$

(b) This type is called nylon-6 because the repeating unit has 6 carbon atoms.

Exercise 7

A could be made from monomer 2. Homopolymer.
B could be made from monomers 1 and 3. Copolymer.
C could be made from monomer 4. Homopolymer.

Exercise 8

E.

Exercise 9

(a) $HOCH_2CH_2OH + HO_2C—\bigcirc—CO_2H + HOCH_2CH_2OH \rightarrow 2H_2O + HOCH_2CH_2—O—C(=O)—\bigcirc—C(=O)—O—CH_2CH_2OH$

(b) Two ester linkages are formed by condensation between —OH and —CO_2H groups.

(c) Terylene (polyethylene terephthalate) is formed by repeated condensation reactions.

Exercise 14 (cont.)

(e) The element sulphur can be used in a hot vulcanization process but a cold process using disulphur dichloride, S_2Cl_2, is more often employed.

(f) The presence of double bonds allows addition reactions to occur so that links can be made between neighbouring chains.

(g) A small degree of cross-linking makes the rubber elastic, i.e. the chains can move relative to one another when pulled, but return to their original positions. As the extent of cross-linking increases, the rubber becomes stiffer until, at 30-50% sulphur content, the structure becomes rigid and hard (ebonite and vulcanite).

Exercise 15

(a) A thermoplastic (or thermosoftening) polymer is one which softens on heating and sets again on cooling. This enables the polymer to be moulded and remoulded into a variety of shapes.

(b) A thermosetting polymer retains its shape on heating. Moulding has to be done at an early stage in production before the rigid structure is achieved by the application of heat.

(c) A typical thermosetting plastic is Bakelite. (Others include carbamide-methanal, melamine-methanal, polyurethanes, etc.)

(d) During thermosetting, cross-links are introduced between adjacent polymer chains giving a rigid structure unaffected by further heating. Cross-linking can occur when a monomer unit has more than two reactive sites at which polymerization is possible.

Exercise 16

(a) X-ray diffraction reveals the crystalline nature of some polymers.

(b)   (i) A regular 'head-to-tail' arrangement of monomer units favours the formation of crystallites (but other factors may override this one).

  (ii) Atactic polymers have a random arrangement of attached groups so that regular crystalline packing is unlikely.

  (iii) Large groups attached to a polymer chain make regular packing difficult. Consequently, crystalline character is low.

  (iv) Extensive chain-branching makes regular packing difficult and is therefore associated with low crystalline character.

  (v) Extensive cross-linking is usually in random directions so that regular packing of polymer chains is unlikely and crystalline character is low.

  (vi) Thermosetts have extensive cross-linking and, therefore, little crystalline character.

(c) Long unbranched polyethene chains are able to pack together fairly closely to give a high degree of crystallinity. The closer packing results in higher density, higher melting-point, greater strength and more rigidity.

Exercise 10

1, 2 and 3, but not 4.

Exercise 11

(a) [benzene ring with OH] $+$ CH_2O $\rightarrow$ [benzene ring with OH and CH_2OH]   Similarly in the 3 and 5 positions

(b) Electrophilic attack. The benzene ring in phenol is particularly susceptible to electrophilic attack because of the activating effect of the —OH group. The carbon atom in methanal has a partial positive charge because it is attached to a highly electronegative oxygen atom; this is a factor in making methanal an electrophile.

(c) [benzene ring with OH, $HOCH_2$, CH_2OH] $+$ [benzene ring with OH, $HOCH_2$, CH_2OH] $+$ [benzene ring with OH, CH_2OH] $+$ [benzene ring with OH, $HOCH_2$, CH_2OH, CH_2OH]

Exercise 12

[$HOCH_2$, benzene ring with OH, CH_2OH] $+$ [benzene ring with OH, CH_2OH] $\rightarrow$ [cross-linked structure of benzene rings with OH, CH_2 bridges, $HOCH_2$, CH_2OH] $+$ $2H_2O$

Exercise 13

Bakelite, once it has been extensively cross-linked, consists of a rigid three-dimensional giant structure in which all the bonds are fairly strong. Hardly any deformation can occur without breaking some of these bonds – consequently, the substance is hard and brittle. For the same reason, solvent molecules cannot penetrate the structure and surround discrete molecules.

Exercise 14

(a) $CH_2{=}C{-}CH{=}CH_2$
        $|$
       CH_3

(b) $-CH_2{-}C{=}CH{-}CH_2-$ repeated indefinitely in a long chain
          $|$
        CH_3

(c) Natural rubber is an addition polymer and a homopolymer.

(d) In vulcanization, neighbouring chains become linked together at intervals by 'bridges' consisting of two or more sulphur atoms.

Exercise 19

(a) Fats are esters derived from propane-1,2,3-triol, commonly called glycerol. The prefix 'tri-' indicates that all three hydroxyl groups have been esterified with a carboxylic acid.

(b)

$$
\begin{array}{l}
|-CH_2-OCOR_1 \qquad \quad CH_2OH \qquad R_1CO_2^-Na^+ \\
|-CH-OCOR_2 + 3NaOH(aq) \rightarrow CHOH + R_2CO_2^-Na^+ \\
|-CH_2-OCOR_3 \qquad \quad CH_2OH \qquad R_3CO_2^-Na^+
\end{array}
$$

Exercise 20

(a) Saturated fats have higher melting-points than unsaturated ones, most of which are oils. Many saturated fats are solids at room temperature.

(b) Oleic and linoleic acids are unsaturated and would therefore be expected in high proportion in unsaturated fats. Similarly, palmitic and stearic acids would be expected in saturated fats.

(c) Animal fats tend to contain a higher proportion of saturated fatty acids. These give glycerides with regularly-shaped side chains which fit together readily to give a solid crystalline structure. The melting-point is normally above room temperature. Vegetable oils, however, contain a large proportion of unsaturated fatty acids. The large irregularly-shaped triglyceride molecules are unable to pack together to form crystalline structures. They are normally liquid at room temperature and form semi-solid slurries on cooling.

Exercise 21

(a) Soaps are rather ineffective and wasteful in hard water because they react with dissolved calcium and magnesium ions to form precipitates (called 'scum') such as calcium stearate (calcium octadecanoate), $(C_{17}H_{35}CO_2^-)_2Ca^{2+}$. Soapless detergents do not form scums in hard water because the corresponding calcium and magnesium salts are soluble.

Soaps do not work in acidic conditions or in sea-water. Hydrogen ions cause precipitation of the free acid, and sodium ions cause precipitation of the soap by the common ion effect.

Soaps tend to be more expensive (for equivalent effects) because they are made from refined animal and vegetable fats whereas soapless detergents are made from the by-products of oil-refining. (The comparison may change as oil becomes more expensive.)

(b) The hydrocarbon 'tails' of early detergents consisted of branched-chain polypropenes which are resistant to bacterial attack. They emerged unchanged from sewage works causing damage to wildlife and often giving rise to masses of dirty foam in rivers and on sea-shores. Most detergents are now biodegradable; the hydrocarbon 'tails' are either unbranched or have a single short branch and these are more readily broken down by bacteria.

Exercise 17

Both polypropenenitrile (in its isotactic form) and nylon have polymer chains which can be readily packed together in crystallites. When the material is drawn into a fibre, these crystalline areas become aligned with the axis of the fibre like logs floating down a river. Parallel fibres are then held together by hydrogen bonding (in nylon) or dipole attraction (in polypropenenitrile).

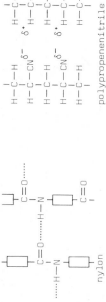

nylon   polypropenenitrile

Polyphenylethene is usually made by a method which results in an isotactic structure. This, coupled with the fact that the attached phenyl groups are bulky, makes the close alignment of polymer chains in fibres difficult to achieve. Consequently, fibres tend to be very weak.

Polyethene can form fibres in which polymer chains are closely aligned but the bonding forces between chains are too weak to form a useful fibre.

Exercise 18

(a) (i) Alkylation (Friedel-Crafts reaction).

 (ii) Dehydrogenation.

(b) (i) $AlCl_3$ as a catalyst; 90-100 °C.

 (ii) ZnO or Fe_2O_3 as a catalyst; 600-630 °C.

(c) A peroxide such as di(benzenecarbonyl) peroxide (benzoyl peroxide), $C_6H_5CO-O-O-COC_6H_5$.

Exercise 24 (continued)

(c) (i) Aminoethanoic acid,

    (ii) 2-aminopropanoic acid,

    (iii) 2-amino-3-hydroxypropanoic acid,

    (iv) 2-amino-3-phenylpropanoic acid,

    (v) 2,6-diaminohexanoic acid,

    (vi) 2-amino-3-methylbutanoic acid.

(d) Systematic names are not used because they are much longer and not simple to abbreviate.

(e) Glycine is the only amino acid of those listed which would not be optically active. It does not contain an asymmetric carbon atom and hence would not exist as enantiomers.

Exercise 25

Glycine exists in the solid state as an 'internal salt', consisting of doubly-charged zwitterion particles, $NH_3^+CH_2CO_2^-$. The strong attraction of these particles for each other leads to a high melting-point, characteristic of ionic compounds. The other three compounds in the table are all covalent liquids and their particles are held together by weak van der Waals forces. There is some hydrogen bonding in 1-aminobutane and propanoic acid, which gives these compounds higher melting-points than methyl ethanoate but the attractive forces are, nevertheless, far weaker than in ionic compounds.

Exercise 26

(a) $CH_3\underset{\underset{NH_2}{|}}{C}HCO_2H(aq) + NaOH(aq) \rightarrow CH_3\underset{\underset{NH_2}{|}}{C}HCO_2^-Na^+(aq) + H_2O(l)$

(b) $CH_3\underset{\underset{NH_2}{|}}{C}HCO_2H(aq) + HCl(aq) \rightarrow CH_3\underset{\underset{NH_3^+Cl^-}{|}}{C}HCO_2H(aq)$

Exercise 27

(a) Form C would predominate at low pH. There is a high concentration of hydrogen ions so that the equilibrium would move to the right (as written).

Form A would predominate at high pH. The concentration of hydrogen ions is low which would cause the equilibrium to move to the left (as written).

(b) B is a zwitterion.
A is the conjugate base of the zwitterion.
C is the conjugate acid of the zwitterion.

(c) Form B, the zwitterion, would show no net movement in an electric field as it would be equally attracted to both electrodes.

Exercise 22

(a) Detergent molecules arrange themselves at the water surface with the polar 'heads' in the water and the non-polar 'tails' pointing upwards. This arrangement breaks up the network of hydrogen bonding between water molecules and therefore reduces the surface tension.

Detergent molecules in excess of the monolayer are arranged in 'micelles', in which the non-polar 'tails' point towards the centre of a sphere with the polar 'heads' at the outside.

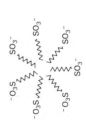

A detergent micelle

(b) The non-polar 'tails' of the detergent molecules are attracted to a grease-spot on a piece of material. They penetrate the grease, leaving their polar 'heads' in contact with the water. The mutual repulsion of the polar 'heads' forces the surface into a spherical shape and a micelle can then leave the surface of the material. The grease globule becomes effectively soluble because it is surrounded by polar 'heads' which interact with water molecules.

(a) Detergent molecules approach grease spot on material

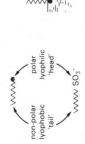

(b) Detergent molecules begin to force grease spot into spherical shape

(c) Grease trapped in water-soluble micelle

Exercise 23

(a), (c) and (d) are anionic detergents. (b) and (e) are cationic.

Exercise 24

(a) All contain an amino group and a carboxyl group attached to the same carbon atom. (Proline has an —NH group instead of an —NH₂ group.)

(b) The letter α shows that the amino group is attached to the carbon atom nearest to the carboxyl group.

(The use of Greek letters has been largely superseded by a numerical system, but note that α becomes 2 and not 1 because 1 refers to the carbon atom in the carboxyl group.)

$$\underset{4}{\overset{\gamma}{C}}-\underset{3}{\overset{\beta}{C}}-\underset{2}{\overset{\alpha}{C}}-\underset{1}{C}O_2H$$

Exercise 30

(a) (i) Alanine is a 'neutral' amino acid since it has one acidic group and one basic group. Consequently, the zwitterion, $CH_3CH(NH_3^+)CO_2^-$, predominates at pH = 7. When acid is added, this form accepts protons and is progressively converted into the acid form, $CH_3CH(NH_3^+)CO_2H$, the change being virtually complete when pH = 1.5.

$$CH_3CH(NH_3^+)CO_2^-(aq) + H^+(aq) \rightleftharpoons CH_3CH(NH_3^+)CO_2H(aq)$$

At a pH of 2.4, i.e. when pH = pK_1, the two forms are present in equal concentrations because:

$$pH = pK_1 - \log \frac{[\text{acid form}]}{[\text{base form}]}$$

(Here, the zwitterion behaves as a base.)

When alkali is added to the neutral solution, the zwitterion gives up protons and is progressively converted into the basic form, $CH_3CH(NH_2)CO_2^-$, the change being virtually complete when pH = 11.5.

$$CH_3CH(NH_3^+)CO_2^-(aq) \rightleftharpoons CH_3CH(NH_2)CO_2^-(aq) + H^+(aq)$$

At a pH of 9.7, i.e. pH = pK_2, the basic form and the zwitterion are present in equal concentrations because:

$$pH = pK_2 - \log \frac{[\text{acid form}]}{[\text{base form}]}$$

(In this reaction, the zwitterion behaves as an acid.)

(b) Lysine has two basic groups and one acidic group. Consequently, there are three pK values, corresponding to the changes:

$NH_3^+(CH_2)_4CH(NH_3^+)CO_2H$	ACIDIC FORM	(Note that CO_2H loses a
	$pK_1 = 2.2$	proton more readily
$\pm H^+\uparrow\downarrow$		than NH_3^+ and that the
$NH_3^+(CH_2)_4CH(NH_3^+)CO_2^-$	ZWITTERION 1	NH_3^+ nearest the CO_2^-
	$pK_2 = 9.0$	loses a proton more
$\pm H^+\uparrow\downarrow$		readily than the
$NH_3^+(CH_2)_4CH(NH_2)CO_2^-$	ZWITTERION 2	farther NH_3^+ does.)
	$pK_3 = 10.5$	
$\pm H^+\uparrow\downarrow$		
$NH_2(CH_2)_4CH(NH_2)CO_2^-$	BASIC FORM	

At a pH of 7, lysine is predominantly in the zwitterion 1 form. Addition of acid converts it progressively to the acidic form, the change being virtually complete when pH = 1.5. Addition of alkali converts zwitterion 1 to zwitterion 2 and then to the basic form, the change being virtually complete when pH = 11.5. By application of the equation:

$$pH = pK - \log \frac{[\text{acid form}]}{[\text{base form}]}$$

we see that the following relationships hold:

at pH = 2.2   [ACIDIC FORM] = [ZWITTERION 1]

at pH = 9.0   [ZWITTERION 1] = [ZWITTERION 2]

at pH = 10.5   [ZWITTERION 2] = [BASIC FORM]

(Continued on page 89.)

Exercise 28

(a) Acidic: aspartic acid and glutamic acid (two acidic groups, one basic).

Basic: lysine and arginine (two basic groups, one acidic).

Neutral: glycine and leucine (one basic group and one acidic).

(b) The isoelectric pH tends to be low for acidic, high for basic and around the neutral point for neutral amino acids.

Exercise 29

(a) At A: $H_3N^+CH_2CO_2H$

At C: $H_3N^+CH_2CO_2^-$

At E: $H_2NCH_2CO_2^-$

(b) Point B on the curve is at pH 2.34, i.e. pH = pK_1. pK_1 refers to the equilibrium:

$$\underset{\text{acid}}{H_3N^+CH_2CO_2H(aq)} \rightleftharpoons \underset{\text{base}}{H_3N^+CH_2CO_2^-(aq)} + H^+(aq)$$

and $pH = pK_1 - \log \frac{[\text{acid form}]}{[\text{base form}]}$

Since pH = pK_1, $\log \frac{[\text{acid form}]}{[\text{base form}]} = 0$

$\therefore$ [acid form] = [base form]

i.e. at point B there are equal concentrations of $H_3N^+CH_2CO_2H$ and $H_3N^+CH_2CO_2^-$.

Point D on the curve is at pH 10.60, i.e. pH = $pK_2 + 1$

pK_2 refers to the equilibrium:

$$\underset{\text{acid}}{H_3N^+CH_2CO_2^-(aq)} \rightleftharpoons H_2NCH_2CO_2^-(aq) + H^+(aq)$$

and $pH = pK_2 - \log \frac{[\text{acid form}]}{[\text{base form}]}$

Since pH = $pK_2 + 1$, $\log \frac{[\text{acid form}]}{[\text{base form}]} = -1$

$\therefore$ [base form] = [base form]

i.e. at point D, $H_2NCH_2CO_2^-$ and $H_3N^+CH_2CO_2^-$ are present in the ratio 10:1.

(c) Glycine would act as a good buffer when sufficient acid or alkali has been added to convert half of it to the acidic or basic forms respectively, i.e. at pH = pK_1 and pK_2. The curve shows that near the points B and D, the pH changes least for the addition of a given amount of acid or alkali.

Glycine is a very poor buffer at pH values around its isoelectric point. Here, there is a very large change in pH for small additions of acid or alkali.

Exercise 30 (continued)

(c) The pK_a values for aspartic acid refer to the changes:

$CO_2HCH_2CH(NH_3^+)CO_2H$ ACIDIC FORM

   $\updownarrow H^+$ $pK_1 = 2.1$

$CO_2^-CH_2CH(NH_3^+)CO_2H$ ZWITTERION 1

   $\updownarrow H^+$ $pK_2 = 3.9$

$CO_2^-CH_2CH(NH_3^+)CO_2^-$ ZWITTERION 2

   $\updownarrow H^+$ $pK_3 = 9.8$

$CO_2^-CH_2CH(NH_2)CO_2^-$ BASIC FORM

At pH = 1, the acidic form, $CO_2HCH_2CH(NH_3^+)CO_2H$, predominates.

At pH = 7, the zwitterion, $CO_2^-CH_2CH(NH_3^+)CO_2^-$, predominates.

At pH = 13, the basic form, $CO_2^-CH_2CH(NH_2)CO_2^-$, predominates.

Exercise 31

(a) $CH_3\underset{\underset{NH_2}{|}}{C}HCO_2H + HONO \rightarrow CH_3\underset{\underset{OH}{|}}{C}HCO_2H + N_2 + H_2O$

(b) (i) An acyl chloride, e.g. ethanoyl chloride, CH_3COCl, or a carboxylic acid anhydride, e.g. ethanoic anhydride, $(CH_3CO)_2O$, could be used to acylate glycine.

(ii) $CH_3\underset{\underset{NH_2}{|}}{C}HCO_2H + CH_3COCl \rightarrow CH_3\underset{\underset{NHCOCH_3}{|}}{C}HCO_2H + HCl$

(c) (i) $CH_3\underset{\underset{NH_2}{|}}{C}HCO_2H + C_2H_5OH \rightarrow CH_3\underset{\underset{NH_2}{|}}{C}HCO_2C_2H_5 + H_2O$

(ii) Dry hydrogen chloride is a suitable catalyst (giving the salt form of the product, $RNH_3^+Cl^-$).

Exercise 32

G = glycine, $CH_2(NH_2)CO_2H$ (or $CH_2(NH_3^+)CO_2^-$)

H = methylamine, CH_3NH_2

I = hydroxyethanoic acid, CH_2OHCO_2H

The high melting-point of G and its solubility in water suggests an ionic compound. The formation of crystalline salts with both acids and bases suggests an amino acid. This is partly confirmed by decarboxylation with soda-lime yielding H, which could be an amine since simple amines burn readily in air and dissolve in water to give alkalis. Further confirmation is given by the reaction of nitrous acid with G, which replaces the —NH_2 group by an —OH group and releases nitrogen and water.

If the amino acid is represented by $R(NH_2)CO_2H$, the compound I is $R(OH)CO_2H$. The relative molecular mass of R is therefore $76-(48+12+2) = 14$, which corresponds to the formula CH_2. The equations for the reactions are as follows:

Exercise 32 (continued)

$CH_2(NH_2)CO_2H(aq) \rightarrow H^+(aq) + CH_2(NH_3^+)CO_2H(aq)$

$CH_2(NH_2)CO_2H(aq) + OH^-(aq) \rightarrow CH_2(NH_2)CO_2^-(aq) + H_2O(l)$

$CH_2(NH_2)CO_2H(s) + 2NaOH(s) \rightarrow CH_2(NH_2)CO_2^-(aq) + H_2O(l) + Na_2CO_3(s)$

$2CH_3NH_2(g) + 4\tfrac{1}{2}O_2(g) \rightarrow N_2(g) + 2CO_2(g) + 5H_2O(g)$

$CH_3NH_2(g) + H_2O(l) \rightarrow CH_3NH_3^+(aq) + OH^-(aq)$

$CH_2(NH_2)CO_2H(aq) + HONO(aq) \rightarrow CH_2(OH)CO_2H(aq) + N_2(g) + H_2O(l)$

Experiment 1.   Questions

1. The solution would be slightly alkaline. Since CO_3^{2-} is the conjugate base of the weak acid HCO_3^- which is, in turn, the conjugate base of the weak acid H_2CO_3, the following equilibria would be set up:

$CO_3^{2-}(aq) + H^+(aq) \rightleftharpoons HCO_3^-(aq)$

$HCO_3^-(aq) + H^+(aq) \rightleftharpoons H_2CO_3(aq)$

These would decrease the concentration of hydrogen ions in solution, making it slightly alkaline.

2. In alkaline solution, the zwitterion form of glycine would tend to lose a proton and become the basic form:

$CH_3NH_3^+CO_2^-(aq) + OH^-(aq) \rightleftharpoons CH_2NH_2CO_2^-(aq) + H_2O(l)$

3. The basic form of glycine can make two bonds, using the lone pair of electrons on the nitrogen and the negative charge on the carboxyl oxygen.

Glycine is therefore a bidentate ligand.

Exercise 33

(a)

(b) This structure would be essentially square planar and would have no net charge.

(Note that this complex is sometimes called a salt because it arises from the combination of two ions.)

Exercise 34

(a)

$$CH_3CO_2H \xrightarrow[\text{u.v. light}]{Cl_2} CH_2ClCO_2H \xrightarrow[\text{conc. aq.}]{NH_3} CH_2NH_2CO_2^-NH_4^+ \xrightarrow{H^+(aq)} CH_2NH_3^+CO_2^-$$

(b)

$$CH_3CHO \xrightarrow[\text{aq}]{KCN,NH_4Cl} \left[\begin{array}{c} OH \\ CH_3-C-H \\ NH_2 \end{array} \rightarrow \begin{array}{c} CN \\ CH_3-C-H \\ NH_2 \end{array} \right] \xrightarrow[\text{reflux}]{H^+(aq)} \begin{array}{c} CO_2H \\ CH_3-C-H \\ NH_2 \end{array}$$

(c) Glycine is not optically active since its molecule has a plane of symmetry – there is no asymmetric carbon atom. Alanine is optically active because of the asymmetric carbon atom. However, in the reaction shown in (b), both enantiomers are formed to give a racemic mixture which is not active.

Exercise 35

(a)

$$\begin{array}{c} CH_3 \\ CH_3-C-H \\ NH_2 \end{array} \begin{array}{c} O \\ C \\ OH \end{array} + \begin{array}{c} H \\ N-H \\ H \end{array} \begin{array}{c} CH_3 \\ C-H \\ C=O \end{array} \rightarrow NH_2-C-N-C-CO_2H + H_2O$$

(b) In aqueous solution, alanine exists primarily as a zwitterion in which the functional groups are not $-NH_2$ and $-CO_2H$ but $-NH_3^+$ and $-CO_2^-$. These groups do not undergo condensation reactions. Even if $-NH_2$ and $-CO_2H$ groups were present, they would be more likely to react by proton transfer (to give $-NH_3^+$ and $-CO_2^-$) than by condensation.

(c) If the $-CO_2H$ group in alanine is converted to a $-COCl$ group by reaction with phosphorus pentachloride, PCl_5, or sulphur oxide chloride, $SOCl_2$, a zwitterion cannot be formed by proton transfer. A condensation reaction readily occurs between the acyl chloride and another alanine molecule.

$$\begin{array}{c} CH_3 \\ CH_3-C-H \\ NH_2 \end{array} \begin{array}{c} O \\ C \\ Cl \end{array} + \begin{array}{c} H \\ N- \\ H \end{array} \begin{array}{c} CH_3 \\ C-H \\ C=O \end{array} \rightarrow NH_2-C-C-N-C-CO_2H + HCl$$

(Long chains will be formed as well. If the dimer alone is required, it is necessary to protect the $-NH_2$ group in half the alanine by acylation before introducing the $-COCl$ group.)

(d) The systematic name is too long and clumsy for regular use and the traditional name is well-established. Moreover, the traditional name suggests how it might be made. Alanylalanine is an example of a dipeptide.

Exercise 36

(a) The central $C-N$ bond is 0.132 nm long which is intermediate between the lengths of single and double bonds. This suggests that the bond has some double bond character due to overlap between the p-orbitals of the lone pair on the N atom and those of the $C=O$ double bond.

(b) There will be restricted rotation about the central $C-N$ bond.

(c)

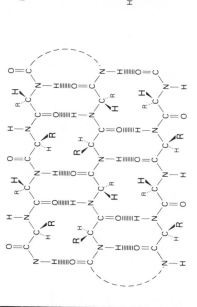

Exercise 37

(a)

α-helix structure of a protein

β-pleated-sheet structure of a protein

(b) The R groups project outwards from the peptide links, roughly at right angles to the main axis of the chain.

Exercise 38

(a) α-helical structure appears in the following ranges of residue numbers.
7-14, 25-35, 80-85, 91-99, 109-115, 119-125.

(b) (i) Cysteine.

(ii)
$$HC-CH_2-SH + HS-CH_2-CH + \tfrac{1}{2}O_2 \rightarrow HC-CH_2-S-S-CH_2-CH + H_2O$$

(iii) The conversion of cysteine to cystine is an oxidation reaction.

(c) Ionic bonding.

$$HCOCH_2CO_2H + NH_2(CH_2)_4CH \rightarrow HCOCH_2CO_2^-NH_3^+(CH_2)_4CH$$

(d) In the denaturing (denaturation) of a protein such as lysozyme, the secondary and tertiary structures are destroyed, leaving the primary structure unaffected. Denaturing may be achieved in a number of ways, e.g. by heating above 70 °C, by the action of strong acids or alkalis and by dissolving in some organic solvents.

Experiment 2. Questions

1. The intensity of the purple (or pink) colour is related to the concentration of the protein. A colorimeter or spectrophotometer could be calibrated to enable concentration to be determined from colour intensity.

2. [biuret–copper complex structure]

3. No, because the biuret complex is formed from nitrogen in peptide bonds. However, care is needed because some amino acids form bluish complexes with copper(II) ions (see Experiment 1) and the colours can be confused.

Exercise 39

(a) [structure of 1-fluoro-2,4-dinitrobenzene]

(b)
$$O_2N\text{–}C_6H_3(NO_2)\text{–}F + NH_2\text{–}CH(CH_3)\text{–}CO_2H \rightarrow O_2N\text{–}C_6H_3(NO_2)\text{–}NH\text{–}CH(CH_3)\text{–}CO_2H + HF$$
2,4-dinitrophenylalanine

(c) The hydrolysis-resistant bond allows the N-terminal end of the peptide chain to be identified. For instance, if alanine were the N-terminal amino acid, treatment with FDNB followed by hydrolysis would yield a yellow compound, 2,4-dinitrophenylalanine (DNP-ala). By chromatography, this can be separated from the other amino acids and identified.

Exercise 40

Item (d) shows that lysine is the N-terminal amino acid, because FDNB reacts selectively with terminal —NH₂ groups. Item (b) shows that lysine is linked to valine, valine to glycine, glycine to glycine and, finally, glycine to arginine:

N   C
lys-val-gly-gly-arg

Confirmation of this order is given by item (c). The amount of pentapeptide is given by

$$n = \frac{m}{M} = \frac{1.00\ \text{g}}{501\ \text{g mol}^{-1}} = 2.00 \times 10^{-3}\ \text{mol}$$

Carboxypeptidase releases amino acids progressively from the C-terminal end, giving an equal amount of arginine and twice as much glycine.

Exercise 41

The peptide is first hydrolyzed by refluxing with 6 M HCl for about 20 hours. Excess acid is removed by evaporation on a steam bath and the solid residue is dissolved in a little warm water. The amino acids are separated and identified by chromatography. (You would be expected to give an account of the technique after you have completed the next section.) The separate spots of amino acids can be re-dissolved from the chromatography paper (or thin-layer adsorbant), evaporated to dryness and weighed to give their relative amounts.

The structure of a dipeptide can be determined by means of its reaction with 1-fluoro-2,4-dinitrobenzene (FDNB), which combines with the terminal —NH₂ group. Subsequent hydrolysis yields one amino acid and one dinitrophenyl amino acid, and these can be identified by chromatography to give the structure of the dipeptide.

The two dipeptides are gly-ala and ala-ala. Since there is no ala-gly, the sequence must be:

N   C
gly-ala-ala-ala

Exercise 42

(a) Table 6

Type of chromatography	Separation phases		Principle* - adsorption or partition
	Mobile	Stationary	
Column	Liquid	Solid	Adsorption
Thin layer	Liquid	Solid	Adsorption
Paper	Liquid	Liquid	Partition
Gas-liquid	Gas	Liquid	Partition

*In some cases, both adsorption and partition occur, but one is nearly always predominant.

(b) In thin layer chromatography, a solid such as silica gel, alumina or celite is made into a slurry with water. Glass or plastic plates are dipped into the slurry and dried to give a thin firm layer of solid.

Column chromatography can be carried out with almost any finely-ground, inert solid. Commonly used are silica gel, charcoal, alumina, magnesium or sodium carbonate, starch, talc or sucrose.

(c) (i) The 'activation' of chromatographic materials, such as charcoal, involves the removal of adsorbed substances by means of strong heating.

(ii) Activation promotes adsorption in chromatography so that separation of substances is more readily achieved.

(d) The rate at which a substance moves during chromatography depends on the relative importance of two factors:

(1) its solubility in the mobile phase,

(2) the extent of its adsorption by (or solubility in) the stationary phase.

The fastest-moving substances are those which are very soluble in the mobile phase and weakly adsorbed (or sparingly soluble in) the stationary phase. The opposite properties cause slow movement.

Experiment 3 Specimen results
Results Table 3

Amino acid	Distances travelled/cm		R_f value
	by solvent	by amino acid	
Aspartic acid - alone	7.1	1.1	0.15
- in mixture	6.8	0.9	0.13
Leucine - alone	7.0	5.5	0.79
- in mixture	6.8	5.1	0.75
Lysine - alone	7.1	2.6	0.37
- in mixture	6.8	2.4	0.35

Experiment 3 Questions

1. R_f values vary slightly with local conditions such as temperature, the purity of the solvent, the nature of the chromatography paper, air-pressure and humidity.

2. The greater the solubility of a substance in a particular solvent, the less readily it is retained by the stationary phase and the faster it appears to move. This gives a higher R_f value.

3. Amino acids are readily transferred from moist and/or dirty fingers on to the paper and show up as confusing brown marks when sprayed with ninhydrin solution.

Exercise 43

(a) A. R_f value in phenol $= \dfrac{25.5 \text{ mm}}{59 \text{ mm}} =$ 0.43

R_f value in butan-1-ol/ethanoic acid $= \dfrac{22.5 \text{ mm}}{59 \text{ mm}} =$ 0.38

∴ A is alanine

B. R_f value in phenol $= \dfrac{37.5 \text{ mm}}{59 \text{ mm}} =$ 0.64

R_f value in butan-1-ol/ethanoic acid $= \dfrac{39.5 \text{ mm}}{59 \text{ mm}} =$ 0.67

∴ B is phenylalanine

(b) Glycine must be the N-terminal amino acid.

(c) Amount of polypeptide $= \dfrac{1.00 \text{ g}}{780 \text{ g mol}^{-1}} = 1.28 \times 10^{-3}$ mol

Approximately the same amount of aspartic acid and A were produced together with twice as much serine. Since carboxypeptidase removes amino acids successively from the C-terminal end of the polypeptide, this shows that the four residues at that end are, in any order:
asp, ser, ser, A.

(d) The most likely sequence is (iii).

(i) has two aspartic acid residues and only one serine in the C-terminal quartet.

(ii) has B instead of A in the C-terminal quartet.

(iv) and (v) have asp, ser, ser and A at the N-terminal end.

Exercise 44

1. E   2. D   3. B   4. D   5. C

Exercise 45

(a) D-glucose is an aldose because the $>C=O$ group is at C^1 which makes it an aldehyde.

(b) Glucose is a hexose.

(c) If the $>C=O$ group is at C^2 the sugar is a ketose.

(d) D-fructose is a structural (functional group) isomer of D-glucose. It has the same arrangement at carbon atoms 3 to 6 but the arrangements at C^1 and C^2 are reversed, i.e. at C^1 there is $—CH_2OH$ and at C^2 there is $>C=O$.

(e) The carbon atoms 2, 3, 4 and 5 are asymmetric, giving two possible arrangements at each. Thus, there are $2 \times 2 \times 2 \times 2 = 16$ stereoisomers.

L-glucose has the $—H$ and $—OH$ at C^5 reversed. (Of the 16 stereoisomers, 8 are D- and 8 are L-. The arrangements at carbon atoms 2, 3 and 4 determine the name of the hexose, e.g. galactose, mannose, etc. while the arrangement at C^5 determines whether it is D- or L-.) D-glucose is readily obtainable from natural sources such as cane and beet sugar. L-glucose has to be synthesized. (All natural sugars are D-sugars.)

Exercise 46

(a)

α-D-glucose   β-D-glucose

(b) The $—H$ and $—OH$ groups at C^1 are in reversed positions in α- and β-D-glucose. The two forms are not enantiomers because they are not mirror images. (They are known as <u>anomers</u> and C^1 is the <u>anomeric</u> carbon atom.)

(c) Pure α-D-glucose is dextrorotatory but when it is dissolved in water the extent of the rotation decreases with time until a steady lower value is reached. This corresponds to an equilibrium mixture of the α- and β-forms; β-D-glucose is also dextrorotatory, but much less so than the α-form. The change is known as <u>mutarotation</u>.

(d) Approximately 1%.

(e) The ring forms are sometimes called pyranoses because their structures are related to that of the unsaturated ring compound pyran, C_5H_6O.

Exercise 47

(a)

(b) Fructose forms a five-membered ring because the anomeric link is made between C^5 and the $>C=O$ group, which is at C^2 rather than C^1. The ring contains carbon atoms 2, 3, 4 and 5 and an oxygen atom.

(c)

(d) Yes, α-D-fructose would be expected to undergo mutarotation in the same way as α-D-glucose.

(e) The structure is related to that of the unsaturated ring compound furan, C_4H_4O.

Exercise 48

(a) (i) Two glucose units. (ii) One glucose unit and one fructose.

(b) Condensation between $—OH$ groups in adjacent monomer units could produce maltose and sucrose.

(c)

Results Table 4

	Glucose	Fructose	Sucrose	Maltose	Starch
A. Dehydration					
(a) Action of heat	Melted easily to a clear liquid which became dark & viscous. Steamy gas.		Melted easily to a clear liquid which became dark & viscous. Steamy gas		
(b) Sulphuric acid	Mixture turned black & swelled giving off heat & much steam. Crumbly black solid left. CO_2 & SO_2 detected.		Mixture turned black & swelled giving off heat & much steam. Crumbly black solid left. CO_2 & SO_2 detected.		
B. Oxidation					
(a) Fehling's soln.	Reddish ppt.	Reddish ppt.	No change.	Reddish ppt.	
(b) Tollens' reagent	Silver mirror.	Silver mirror.	No change.	Silver mirror.	
C. Carbonyl derivatives					
(a) 2,4-dinitro-phenylhydrazine	Yellow ppt. (slow)	Yellow ppt. (slow)			
(b) phenylhydrazine	Yellow ppt. 5 mins M.Pt. 205 °C	Yellow ppt. 3 mins M.Pt. 205 °C			
D. Hydrolysis				Red ppt. with Fehling's solution	A & C. Complete hydrolysis to reducing sugar. No starch left. B. Partial hydrolysis.

Exercise 49

(a) Glycogen is the carbohydrate stored in animals' liver. It acts as a short-term reserve food-store as it can be quickly broken down into glucose and passed into the bloodstream.

Amylopectin is the carbohydrate making up the bulk (85%) of starch. It is insoluble in water and acts as a plant food storage material.

Cellulose is the structural carbohydrate found in plant-cell walls. It is the main constituent of cotton, hemp and paper.

(b) (i) Amylose and amylopectin are both polymers made of glucose units joined by α-1,4-links. In amylose, the chains remain unbranched, while in amylopectin they are joined, at intervals, by extra β-1,6-links, resulting in large branched-chain molecules.

(ii) Glycogen, like amylopectin, is a branched polymer of glucose. The main difference is that in glycogen branching occurs more frequently than in amylopectin (about every 12 glucose units).

(iii) In glycogen, glucose units are joined by α-1,4 linkages whereas in cellulose the links are β-1,4. In addition, the glycogen structure branches about every 12 residues while cellulose remains as straight chains. The chains are hydrogen-bonded along their length, however, to form fibrils.

Experiment 4 Specimen results

Results Table 5

		Movement of analyzer from zero		
	Initial	½ volume	Diluted	+ indicates clockwise − indicates anticlockwise
Glucose	+27°	+13°	+13°	
Sucrose				

Time, t/min	0	3	6	10	15	20	30	8
Analyzer reading, α_t/°	+34	+18	+7	− 1	− 8	− 9	−11	−12
$\alpha_t - \alpha_\infty$/°	46	30	19	11	4	3	1	0

94

Exercise 50

(a) The purine bases are adenine and guanine. The pyrimidine bases are thymine and cytosine.

(b)

(c) RNA polynucleotides contain the sugar ribose (not deoxyribose as in DNA), the chains do not form a double helix, and are generally shorter.

Exercise 51

(a) In the saturated fatty acids there is a steady rise in melting-point with increasing chain length. This is to be expected from the increasing van der Waals forces of attraction between similar molecules of increasing size (number of electrons).

In the unsaturated fatty acids a similar increase is seen between palmitoleic and oleic acids but, thereafter, the number of double bonds seems more important than the molecular size. An increase in the number of double bonds decreases the melting-point sharply, even when accompanied by an increase in molar mass, e.g. between linolenic and arachidonic acids. The *cis* configuration makes it very difficult for unsaturated chains to pack closely together and the effect increases with the number of double bonds.

(b) Saturated fatty acids have higher melting-points and are mostly solids at room temperature. Unsaturated fatty acids have lower melting-points and are mostly liquids.

Experiment 4   Questions

1. The main products are carbon and water.

$$C_6H_{12}O_6 \rightarrow 6C + 6H_2O$$

2. The reaction is called dehydration because water molecules are removed.

3. Some of the sulphuric acid is reduced by the hot carbon to sulphur dioxide, while some of the carbon is oxidized to carbon dioxide.

$$C(s) + 2H_2SO_4(l) \rightarrow CO_2(g) + 2SO_2(g) + 2H_2O(l)$$

Some is merely diluted by the water released.

4. In each case, glucose is oxidized to gluconic acid (the —CHO group becomes —CO$_2$H). Tollens' reagent is reduced to metallic silver, and Fehling's solution is reduced to copper(I) oxide.

5. Glucose reduces Tollens' reagent and Fehling's solution because it has an aldehyde group —CHO. Fructose is also a reducing sugar, even though it has no —CHO group; the combination —C—C— is an effective reductant.
$$\overset{\displaystyle \;\;||\;\;\;\;}{\underset{O\;\;\;\;OH}{}}$$

In sucrose, however, the link between the glucose and fructose units is made via the reducing groups which then become ineffective.

6. The product is called glucosazone.

7. $C_{12}H_{22}O_{11} + H_2O \rightarrow C_6H_{12}O_6 + C_6H_{12}O_6$
   sucrose   glucose   fructose

8. Both sucrose and glucose are dextrorotatory; fructose is laevorotatory. The final mixture is dextrorotatory to a greater extent than glucose is dextrorotatory. 'Inversion' refers to the change from dextrorotation to laevorotation, (+) to (−).

9. The inversion of sucrose is catalyzed by invertase.

10. $[\alpha] = \dfrac{\alpha}{lc} \quad \therefore c = \dfrac{\alpha}{[\alpha]l} = \dfrac{27°}{52.5° \text{ cm}^3 \text{ g}^{-1} \text{ dm}^{-1} \times 1 \text{ dm}} = 0.51 \text{ g cm}^{-3}$

11. $\alpha_t - \alpha_\infty$ is proportional to the amount of sucrose present in the solution. The slope of the curve is therefore proportional to the rate of the reaction and this decreases to zero as the reaction proceeds to completion. (This is a good example of a first order reaction – see Unit P5 (Chemical Kinetics).

Exercise 52

(a) Coconut oil   (b) Soybean oil.

(c) Coconut oil has the highest percentage of saturated fatty acids.
(Palm kernel oil, beef tallow, butter and lard are also high in
saturated acids.) Soybean oil has the lowest percentage of saturated
fatty acids.

Exercise 53

Wave motion	Wave length	Array
microwaves	1 – 10 cm	crystal model
pond waves	10 – 30 cm	row of posts
visible light	10^{-4} cm	cloth (fine weave)
X-rays	10^{-6} – 10^{-10} cm	crystal

Exercise 54

(a)

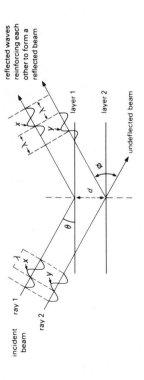

(b) The distances travelled by rays 1 and 2 must differ by a whole number
of wavelengths, i.e.

$$AB + BC = n\lambda$$

but $$AB = BC = d \sin \theta$$

or $$2d \sin \theta = n\lambda \qquad \text{(This is the Bragg equation.)}$$

(c) $\phi = 2\theta$

This is why 2θ appears in Fig. 35 and other similar diagrams, rather
than θ.

(d) Several peaks appear on each trace because reinforcement of the
reflected rays occurs for different values of n. These decrease in
intensity as n increases from 1, although this is not shown clearly in
in Fig. 35.

(e) Three different traces are obtained for three different sets of planes
as the crystal is rotated. These planes are shown in Fig. 33, page 80.

Exercise 55

$n\lambda = 2d \sin \theta$

Assume n = 1 for a fairly strong reflected beam

$$\therefore 0.0583 \text{ nm} = 2d \sin 9°$$

$$= 2d \times 0.156$$

$$\therefore d = \frac{0.0583}{2 \times 0.156} = \boxed{0.187 \text{ nm}}$$

Exercise 56

$\theta = \frac{1}{2}\phi$ (see Fig. 34, page 81).

$$= \frac{1}{2}(47°30')$$

$$= 23°45'$$

$n\lambda = 2d \sin \theta \quad \text{or} \quad d = \dfrac{n\lambda}{2 \sin \theta}$

$$\therefore d = \frac{n \times 0.0635 \text{ nm}}{2 \sin 23°45'} = \frac{n \times 0.0635}{2 \times 0.4027} \text{ nm} = n \times 0.0788 \text{ nm}$$

If n = 1 then d = $\boxed{0.0788 \text{ nm}}$

If n = 2 then d = $\boxed{0.158 \text{ nm}}$

If n = 3 then d = $\boxed{0.236 \text{ nm}}$

The first two values are rather small, compared with the diameters of most
atoms and ions, which makes the third most likely. The best method of
distinguishing them, however, would be to look for other reflected beams at
angles obtained by substituting these values for d into the Bragg equation
using different values of n. For instance, if 0.236 nm is the correct value,
then there should be a brighter beam (n = 2) at θ = $15\frac{1}{2}°$ and a still
brighter beam (n = 1) at θ = 8°. If 0.158 nm is the correct value, then
there should be a brighter beam (n = 1) at θ = $11\frac{1}{2}°$ and a weaker beam
(n = 3) at θ = 37°.

Exercise 57

$2d \sin \theta = n\lambda$

$$\therefore 2 \times 0.198 \text{ nm} \times \sin 12° = 1 \times \lambda$$

i.e. $\lambda = 2 \times 0.198 \text{ nm} \times 0.208 = \boxed{0.0824 \text{ nm}}$

Plastics illustrated in the photograph on page 24

A. Polyethene
1. Bottle on window sill.
2. Butter pack lining.
3. Fruit wrappings.
4. Colander.
5. Baby cups.
6. Boil-in-the-bag sachet.

B. Polychloroethene
7. Plate-rack coating.
8. Kitchen gloves.
9. Telephone wire insulation.
10. Shoes.
11. Flooring.
12. Protectors on high-chair frame.
13. Shopping bag (cloth-backed).
14. High-chair seat cover.

C. Polypropene
15. Pastry mould.
16. Bowl (in plate-rack).
17. Food-mixer casing.
18. Cheese wrap.

D. Polyphenylethene
19. Wall tiles (behind sink).
20. Radio casing.
21. Cream pot.
22. Refrigerator lining.
23. Spice-pot lids.
24. Flower-pots.
25. Venetian-blinds.
26. Kitchen-scales, casing and pan.
27. Insulated cup (expanded poly-phenylethene).

E. Polymethyl 2-methylpropenoate (perspex)
28. Window on kitchen scales.

F. Polyester (Terylene)
29. Sweater.
30. Socks.
31. Net curtains.

G. Polypropenenitrile
32. Skirt.

H. Nylon
33. Gears in food mixer.
34. Tights.

I. Melamine - methanal
35. Table top.
36. Telephone.
37. Work-top.
38. Cupboard facings.

J. Phenol - methanal (PF resin)
39. Kettle handle.

K. Carbamide - methanal (UF resin)
40. Light fitting.

L. Polyurethane
41. Paint on kitchen wall.
42. Padding in high-chair seat.

Exercise 58

(a) The crystal is rotated so that various sets of planes come into position at the correct angle to give reinforcing reflected beams.

(b) The spots (or rings) in X-ray diffraction patterns vary in intensity because atoms with large numbers of electrons (dense electron clouds) diffract X-rays more strongly than those with small numbers of electrons.

(c) Hydrogen atoms have low density electron clouds and therefore diffract X-rays very weakly.

Exercise 59

(a) Covalent bonding. The contours show a significant electron density in the region between neighbouring atoms. This indicates the electron sharing which is characteristic of covalent bonding.

(b) A, H and I are oxygen atoms - they have greater electron density than B, C, D, E, F, G, J and K which are therefore carbon atoms.

(c) Hydrogen atoms cannot be located precisely, but their presence is indicated by the outward projections from the contour of lowest electron density.